The Spirit-Filled LIFE

The Spirit-Filled LIFE

Charles Finney

Whitaker House

THE SPIRIT-FILLED LIFE

ISBN: 0-88368-336-9
Printed in the United States of America
Copyright © 1999 by Whitaker House

Whitaker House
30 Hunt Valley Circle
New Kensington, PA 15068

Library of Congress Cataloging-in-Publication Data

Finney, Charles Grandison, 1792–1875
    The spirit-filled life / by Charles Finney
        p.   cm.
    ISBN 0-88368-336-9 (trade paper)
      1. Evangelistic sermons. 2. Sermons, American. 3. Congregational
churches—Sermons. I. Title
    BV3797.F5413   1999
    252'.058—dc21   99-055606

    1 2 3 4 5 6 7 8 9 10 11 12 13 / 07 06 05 04 03 02 01 00 99

Contents

Preface

❖

The following sermons are only a few of the many preached by Charles Finney at Oberlin College during the years 1845–1861. Few preachers in any age have surpassed Finney in clear and well-defined views of conscience, and of man's moral convictions. Few have been more fully at home in the domain of law and government. Few have learned more of the spiritual life from experience and from observation. Few have discriminated the true from the false more closely, or have been more skillful in speaking forth their points clearly. Hence, these sermons under God were full of spiritual power. They are given to the public in this form, directed toward a reader rather than listeners, in the hope that at least a measure of the same saving power that touched the listeners may bless the reader.

Chapter 1

The Inner and Outer Revelation

By manifestation of the truth commending ourselves to every man's conscience in the sight of God.
—2 Corinthians 4:2

There are many people who feel that unbelief has rarely, if ever, been more prevalent in our country than at this time, especially among young people. I am not prepared to say it is an honest unbelief, yet it may very well be real. Young men and women may really doubt the inspiration of the Christian Scriptures, not because they have honestly studied those Scriptures and their numerous evidences, but because they have read them little and reasoned about them even less. Moreover, they have almost universally failed to study what their own minds intuitively tell them. They have not examined the original revelation that God has made in each human soul, to see how far this will carry them and how wonderfully it opens the way for understanding and for embracing the revelation given in God's Word.

I have taken as my text verse the words of Paul: *"By manifestation of the truth commending ourselves to every man's conscience in the sight of God."* Here, Paul was speaking of the gospel ministry that he received, and he was stating how he fulfilled it. He showed plainly that he sought to preach to the human conscience. He found in each man's soul a conscience to which he could appeal, and to which the manifestation of the truth commended itself.

Probably no thoughtful person has ever read the Bible without noticing that there has been a previous revelation given in some way to mankind. The Bible assumes many things as being already known. When I was studying in my law office, I bought my first Bible as one of my law books. No sooner had I opened it than I was surprised to see how many things it assumes as known, and therefore states with no attempt at proving them. For instance, look at the first verse in the Bible, *"In the beginning God created the heavens and the earth"* (Gen. 1:1). This assumes the existence of God. It does not attempt to prove this truth; it goes on the presumption that this revelation—the existence of God—has been already made to all who are mature enough to understand it.

In his epistle to the Romans, the apostle Paul also asserted that the real Godhead and the eternal power of the one God, though in some sense *"invisible attributes,"* are yet *"clearly seen"* in the creation of the world, *"being understood by the things that are made,"* so that all wicked men are *"without excuse"* (Rom. 1:20). His teaching is that the created universe reveals God. If this is true of the universe around us, it is no less true of the universe within us. The convictions of our own minds truly reveal

God and many of the great truths concerning our relationship to Him and to His government.

When we read the Bible attentively, we notice how many things of the utmost importance it assumes. The Bible bases its precepts on them, without attempting to prove them. Thus, we must inquire, "Are these assumptions properly made?"

The answer to this question is found when we look within ourselves, at what our own minds intuitively affirm to be true. Then we will see that we possess an intellectual and moral nature that reveals great truths concerning God and our relationship to Him and to His law—just as the material world reveals His eternal power and Godhead.

For instance, just as man has a physical nature related to the physical world, we will see that he also has a moral nature related to spiritual and moral truth. As his senses—sight, touch, hearing—perceive certain truths of the external world, so does his spiritual nature perceive certain truths of the spiritual world. No one can carefully consider the first class of truths without being forced to consider and believe the second. Let us see if this is true.

Not long ago, I spoke with a young lady of considerable intelligence who was a skeptic. She claimed to believe in God and in the great truths pertaining to His attributes that are embraced in Deism. But she quite rejected the Bible and all that pertains to a revealed way of salvation.

I began by presenting to her some of the great truths that our own minds affirm concerning God, His attributes, and His government. From here, I went on to show her how the Bible completes the system of truth needed by man as a race of lost sinners.

She admitted the first point, of course. Then she saw that the second must also be true if the first was, or there could be nothing for man but hopeless ruin. Seeing the great gulf of despair, she was horrified and saw that only her unbelief was ruining her soul. She then renounced this, yielded her heart to God, and found gospel peace and joy in believing. I will now present the same ideas here that I presented to her.

God's First Revelation

The first great question is, What ideas does our own nature—God's first revelation—give us?

The Idea of God

Undoubtedly, the inner revelation gives us the idea of God. Our own minds affirm that there is and must be a God, and that He must have all power and all knowledge. Our minds also give us God's moral attributes. No one can doubt that God is good and just. People are never afraid that God will do anything wrong. If they are at all afraid of God, it is because He is good—because He is just and holy.

The Idea of Moral Law

Man's nature gives him the idea of moral law. He can no more doubt the existence of a moral law—imposed on himself—than he can doubt the existence of his own soul and body. He knows that he should not be selfish, that he ought to be benevolent. He knows that he is required to love his neighbor as himself—required to sacrifice the lower good, if need be, in order to seek the higher good.

How do men get these ideas? I answer, They have them by nature; the ideas are in their minds before any direct instruction comes from human lips. Otherwise, you could never teach a child these ideas any more than you could teach them to a horse. The child knows these things before he is taught, and he cannot remember when he first heard them.

Suppose you were to close your Bible and ask, "Apart from everything that this Book teaches, how much do I know? How much must I say is true?" You would find that your moral nature gives you the idea of a God and affirms His existence; it gives you His attributes, natural and moral, and also your own moral relationship to Him and to your fellowmen. As proof of this, not one of you can say, "I am under no obligation to love God; I am not required to love my fellowmen." Your moral nature gives you these things—it affirms these truths to you, even more directly and undeniably than your senses give you the facts of the external world.

Furthermore, your moral nature not only gives you the law of supreme love for God, and of equal and impartial love toward your fellowmen, but it also affirms that you are a sinner. You know that you have displeased God—have utterly failed to please Him— and of course that you are under condemnation from His righteous law. You know that God's good law must condemn you, because you have not been good in the sense required by that law. Hence, you must know that you are an outlaw, condemned by law, and without hope from the administration of justice.

Awareness of Impenitence

Another thing that man's nature gives him is the knowledge that he is still unrepentant. His own conscience affirms this to him beyond all contradiction. If you are impenitent, your nature affirms that you are still living in sin and have not reformed in such a way that God can accept your reformation. You know that you do violence to your own conscience, and that, while you are doing this, you can neither respect yourself nor be respected by God. As long as this is the case with you, you know that God cannot forgive you. Moreover, if He does forgive you, it will do you no good; you could not be happy, you could not respect yourself, even if you were told that you were forgiven. Indeed, if your nature spoke out unbiased while you were still doing violence to your conscience, it would not let you believe that you were really forgiven.

I can remember when these thoughts were in my mind *like fire*. I saw that no man could doubt them, any more than he can doubt his own existence. In the same way, you may see these truths and feel their force.

Therefore, you know that, by your sins, you have forfeited the favor of God and have no claim on Him at all in regard to justice. You have cast off His authority, have disowned subjection to His law and government; indeed, you have cast all His precepts beneath your feet. You can no longer come before God and say, "You should not cast me off; I have not deserved it at Your hand." You can no more say this honestly than you can deny your own existence.

Did you ever think of this? Have you ever tried this, to see what you can honestly do and say before God? Have you ever tried to go into God's presence and tell Him solemnly that He has no right to punish you? Not one of you can tell Him so without being conscious of your blasphemy.

This is a good method, because it may serve to show you how the case really stands. Suppose you try it, then. See what you can honestly say before God, with an approving conscience, when your soul is deeply impressed with the sense of His presence. I am not asking you whether you can harden your heart and violate your conscience enough to blaspheme God to His face. Rather, I am asking you to put the honest convictions of your own conscience to the test and see what they are and what they will allow you to do and say before God. Can you kneel down before Him and say, "God, I deny that I have cast You off. I have never refused to treat You as a friend. I have never treated You as an enemy"? You know that you cannot do anything of the sort without encountering the rebukes of your own mind.

No Hope of Forgiveness under the Law

Again, your own mind tells you that you have no reason to hope for forgiveness under the law. Even with all the light of your Deism, you can discern no grounds for pardon. Apart from the Bible, all is dark as death. There is no hope. If you cherish any hope of forgiveness apart from the Bible, it must be in direct opposition to your own solemn convictions. You can never infer from the goodness of God that He *can* forgive, much less that He *must*.

One of the first Universalist preachers I ever heard speak announced, at the beginning of his sermon, that he believed God would save all men because of His goodness. I clearly remember how perfectly shallow his ideas appeared, and how absurd his assumptions were to me. I was not a Christian then, but I saw at a glance that he might do better to believe that, because of the goodness of God, He would forgive *no one* rather than everyone. It seemed very clear to me that, if God were good and had made a good law, He would sustain it. Why not? God's law must be a good one; how could a Being of infinite wisdom and love impose any law but a good law? And if it is a good law, it has a good purpose to fulfill. A good God cannot allow it to fail in fulfilling that purpose by letting it come to nothing through inefficiency in its administration.

I knew enough about law and government to know that a firm hand in administration is essential to any good results from a law, no matter how good the law may be. Suppose a law were left to be trampled underfoot by hardened, blasphemous transgressors. Then suppose that an indiscriminate pardon were given and nothing were done to sustain the law. In such a case, there would be an end of all authority and a definite annihilation of all the good hoped for under its administration. Considering this, how can a rational individual infer from God's goodness that He will pardon all sinners?

Suppose that a riot erupts in your town. The rioters tear up the train tracks, burn down the bridges, run whole trains off their tracks, and crush the flesh of hundreds en masse into heaps of blood and bones. When the guilty are arrested and convicted by due course of law, the question will come up, Will the mayor pardon them? He might be very much inclined to do so, if he could. But the question is, Can a good mayor do it? Supposing that he is purely good and truly wise, what would he do? Will you say, "Oh, he is too good to punish! He is so good, he will certainly pardon"? If a pardon were indiscriminately given, and given to all, would the highest respect for law and the best obedience be secured? Everybody knows that this is sheer and utter nonsense. No man who ever had any interactions with the responsibilities of government, or who has ever learned the ABCs of human nature in this context, can for one moment suppose that such pardon can replace punishment with any result other than pure ruin. Indeed, if the ruler is good, he will surely punish the rioters; and the more goodness he has in his character, the surer the punishment will be.

You, sinners, are under law. If you sin, you must see great reason why God should punish and not forgive.

The Need for a Second Revelation

Here is another fact. When you look at yourself and your moral position, you find yourself twice dead. You are *civilly* dead, in the sense of being condemned by law, an outcast from the favor of government. You are also *morally* dead, for you do not love God, do not serve Him, have no tendency to be drawn back into sympathy with Him. Rather, you are dead to all careful thought in this direction. You are indeed alive to your own low, selfish interests, but dead to God's interests. You care nothing for God except to avoid Him and escape His judgment. You know all this, beyond all doubt.

In this condition, without a further revelation, where is your hope? You have none, and you have no basis for any.

Furthermore, if a future revelation is to be made, revealing some basis for pardon, you can see with the light now before you that it must come from God. The first revelation shows you that if help ever comes, it cannot come out of yourself, but must come from God. You can see what more you need from Him. Help cannot come from His justice, but must come from His mercy. It cannot come out of law, but must come from some extra provision by which law may have its demands satisfied other than through the penalty being carried out on the offender. Somebody must intervene for you—somebody who can take your part and stand in your place before the offended law.

Did you never think of this? In the position where you now stand, and where your own nature and your own convictions place you, you are compelled to say, "My case is hopeless! I need a double salvation!" You need salvation both from condemnation and from sinning; first from the curse, and second from the tendency to commit sin. If you were to ask for a revelation to meet these needs of your lost soul, where could you find it? Is it to be found in all of nature? No; it is nowhere. Look into the irresistible convictions of your own moral being; they tell you of your needs, but they give you nothing with which to meet those needs. Your own moral nature shows that you need an atoning Savior and a renewing Spirit. Nothing less can meet the case of a sinner condemned, outlawed, and doubly dead by the moral corruption of all his voluntary powers.

The worst harm that unbelief causes is that it ignores all this; it takes no notice of one entire side of our nature—the most important side. Those who do not believe the Gospel talk a great deal about philosophy, yet they restrict themselves to the philosophy of the outer world and have no eye for the inner and higher nature. They ignore the fact that our moral nature affirms an entire class of great truths with even more force and certainty than the senses affirm the facts of the external world. Truly, this is a great and fatal omission!

REMARKS

1. Without the first revelation, the second could not be satisfactorily proved. When the Bible reveals God, it assumes that our minds affirm His existence and that we need no higher proof. When it reveals His law, it presupposes that we are capable of understanding it and of grasping the significance of its moral claims. When it prescribes duty, it assumes that we ought to feel the force of obligation to obey it.

Now, the fact that the Bible does make many assumptions of this kind establishes an intimate connection between the Scriptures and the laws of the human mind. If these assumptions are well and truly made, then the divine authority of the Bible is abundantly sustained by its harmony with the nature of man. It fits the beings to whom it is given, both intellectually and morally. But on the other hand, if these assumptions had proved false, it would be impossible to sustain the credibility of the Scriptures as coming from a wise and honest Being.

2. Having the first revelation, to reject the second is most absurd. The second is, to a great extent, a reaffirmation of the first, with important additions, including the Atonement (and thus the possibility of pardon) and the gift and work of the Spirit (and thus the analogous possibility of being saved from sinning).

Now, the things that the first revelation affirms and the second revelation reaffirms are fundamental in any revelation of moral duty to moral beings. They are so fundamental that, since they are taught so intuitively and undeniably, we can only convict ourselves of extreme absurdity if we then reject the second revelation. Logically, there seem to be no grounds left on which to base a denial of the written revelation. Its supplementary doctrines are certainly not intuitive truths, but they are directly related to man's needs as a lost sinner, and they richly supply those needs. Moreover, they are so beautifully related to the requirements of God's government, and so amply meet them, that no intelligent mind, once understanding all these things in their actual relationships, can fail to recognize their truthfulness.

3. The study of the first revelation brings us to an intellectual reception of the second. If a man will thoroughly examine and understand what his own mind tells him and then come to the Scriptures and properly understand their relationship to his own moral nature, moral convictions, and moral needs, I believe he must be compelled to say, "All of it is true; this Book is all true! They coincide so wondrously, and the former sustains the latter so admirably and so triumphantly, a man can no more deny the Bible

after knowing all his own moral position than he can deny his own existence."

4. You see why so many people reject the Bible. They have not read *themselves* well. They have not looked within, to read carefully the volume that God has put on record there. They have attempted to hush and smother the ever rising convictions of their own moral natures. They have refused to listen to the cry of need that swells up from their troubled souls of guilt. Hence, they are yet strangely ignorant of one whole volume of revelation. This ignorance accounts for their rejection of the Bible.

Suppose I told you the two great precepts of the moral law. Wouldn't their obvious nature and importance cause you to feel that these precepts must be true and must be from God? As I presented more of the precepts' particulars, you would still affirm, "These must be true; these must certainly have come down from heaven." Even if I were to go back to the Mosaic Law (a Law that many people oppose because they do not understand the circumstances that called for such a Law) and to explain the reasons for its statutes, every man would have to affirm the rightness of those statutes. The Old Testament, I am aware, reveals truth under a veil, the world not being prepared then for its clearer revelation. (See 2 Corinthians 3:14–16.) The veil was taken away when, in the fullness of time, people were prepared for unclouded revelations of God in the flesh. (See Galatians 4:4.)

Therefore, the reason why so many people receive the Bible is not that they are gullible and swallow absurdities with ease. Rather, the Bible commends itself so irresistibly to each man's own

nature and to his deep and resistless convictions, he
has no choice but to receive it—he would violate his
inner convictions if he were to reject it. Man's whole
nature cries out, "This is just what I need!"

One young lady with whom I spoke could not
help but abandon her unbelief and yield up her heart
to God when she had reached this point. I said, "Do
you admit that there is a God?" She answered,
"Yes." "Do you admit that there is a law?" "Yes."
"Do you admit to your personal guilt?" "Yes." "And
your need of salvation?" "Oh, yes." I then asked,
"Can you help yourself?" She said, "Ah, no, indeed. I
do not believe I can ever be saved." "But God can
save you. Surely nothing is too hard for Him," I told
her. (See Jeremiah 32:17, 27.) She replied, "My own
nature has bound me. I am in despair; there is no
way of escape for me. You know, I don't believe the
Bible, and here I am in darkness and despair!"

At this point I began to speak of the Gospel. I
said to her, "God has come down and dwelt in human flesh to meet the case of such sinners as you
are. He has made an ample atonement for sin. What
do you think of that?" "That is exactly what I need,"
she said, "if it were only true." "If it is not true," I
said, "you are lost beyond hope! Then why not believe?" "I cannot believe it," she said, "because it is
incredible. It is a great deal too good to be true!"
"And isn't God *good,*" I said, "infinitely good? Then
why do you object that anything He does is too good
to be true?" "That is what I need," she repeated,
"but how can it be so?" "Then you cannot give God
credit for being so good!" I said. She replied, "Oh, I
see it is my unbelief! But I cannot believe. It is what
I need, I can plainly see; but how can I believe it?"

The Inner and Outer Revelation

At this point I rose up and said to her solemnly, "The crisis has come! There is now only one question for you: Will you believe the Gospel?" She raised her eyes, which had been covered for half an hour or more. Every feature showed the most intense agitation. I repeated, "Will you believe God? Will you give Him credit for sincerity?" At that moment, the young lady threw herself upon her knees and burst into loud weeping. What a scene—to see a skeptic beginning to give her God credit for love and truth! To see the door of light and hope opened, and heaven's blessed light breaking in upon a desolate soul! Have you ever witnessed such a scene? When this young woman next opened her lips, it was to praise her Savior!

The Bible assumes that you have enough light to see, to do your duty, and to find the way to heaven. A great many of you are perhaps bewildered in regard to your religious opinions, believing in loose and skeptical ideas. You have not seen that it is the most reasonable thing in the world to acknowledge and embrace this glorious truth. Will you allow yourself to go on, bewildered, without considering that you are yourself a living, walking revelation of truth? Will you refuse to come into a relationship with God and Christ that will save your soul?

In my early years, when I was tempted to skepticism, I can well remember that I said to myself, "It is much more probable that ministers and the multitudes of good men who believe the Bible are right, than that I am right. They have examined the subject, but I have not. It is therefore entirely unreasonable for me to doubt."

There is no reason why you should not say, "I know the Gospel is suited to my needs. I know I am afloat on the vast ocean of life, and if there is no Gospel, there is nothing that can save me. It is therefore doing no good for me to stand here and raise frivolous objections. I must examine this matter. I can at least see that if God offers me mercy, I must not reject it." Doesn't this Gospel show you how you can be saved from hell and from sin? Oh, then, believe it! Let the blessed truth find a heart open to it. When you dare to give God credit for all His love and truth, and when you bring your heart under the power of this truth and yield yourself up to its blessed influence, that will be the dawn of morning to your soul! *"Whoever desires, let him take the water of life freely"* (Rev. 22:17).

Chapter 2

The Savior Lifted Up

*And as Moses lifted up the serpent in the wilderness,
even so must the Son of Man be lifted up, that whoever
believes in Him should not perish but have eternal life.*
—John 3:14–15

*And I, if I am lifted up from the earth,
will draw all peoples to Myself.*
—John 12:32

*So the LORD sent fiery serpents among the people, and
they bit the people; and many of the people of Israel died.
Therefore the people came to Moses, and said, "We have
sinned, for we have spoken against the LORD and against
you; pray to the LORD that He take away the serpents from
us." So Moses prayed for the people. Then the LORD said to
Moses, "Make a fiery serpent, and set it on a pole; and it
shall be that everyone who is bitten, when he looks at it,
shall live." So Moses made a bronze serpent, and put it on
a pole; and so it was, if a serpent had bitten anyone, when
he looked at the bronze serpent, he lived.*
—Numbers 21:6–9

When Christ, in John 12:32, alluded to Moses
lifting up the serpent, He was referring to this
passage in Numbers 21. In both cases, the

purpose was to save men from perishing. When the effects of the serpent's bite go unchecked, it means the death of the body; and when sin is left unpardoned and uncleansed from the heart, it spells the ruin of the soul. Christ is lifted up so that sinners, believing in Him, *"should not perish but have eternal life."*

In this context, *"perish"* cannot mean annihilation. Rather, it must be the opposite of *"eternal life,"* which is clearly much more than eternal existence. Eternal life must be eternal happiness—real life in the sense of exquisite enjoyment. The counterpart of this, eternal misery, falls under the term *"perish."* It is common in the Scriptures to find a state of endless misery contrasted with one of endless happiness.

In examining this subject, we may observe two points of similarity between the bronze serpent and Christ.

First, Christ must be lifted up as the serpent was in the wilderness. Look more closely at the passage from John 12: *"'And I, if I am lifted up from the earth, will draw all peoples to Myself.' This He said, signifying by what death He would die"* (vv. 32–33). It is obvious that this refers to Christ's being raised up from the earth upon His cross at His crucifixion.

Second, Christ must be held up as a remedy for sin, even as the bronze serpent was held up as a remedy for a poison. It is not uncommon in the Bible to see sin represented as an illness. For this illness, Christ had healing power. He claimed to be able to forgive sin and to cleanse the soul from its moral pollution. He continually claimed to have this power and encouraged men to rely upon Him and to resort to Him for its application. In all His personal instructions, He was careful to hold Himself up as having this power, and as capable of providing a remedy for sin. (See, for example, Matthew 9:2–7.)

In this respect, the bronze serpent was a type of Christ. Whoever looked upon this serpent was healed. In the same way, Christ heals not only from punishment—for the analogy of healing is less pertinent to this—but also and especially from sinning. He heals the heart from its tendency to sin; He heals the soul and restores it to health. So it was said by the announcing angel, *"You shall call His name JESUS, for He will save His people from their sins"* (Matt. 1:21). His power avails to cleanse and purify the soul.

Christ, Our Remedy

A Full and Adequate Remedy

Both Christ and the bronze serpent were held up as a remedy, and let it be noted that both were held up as a full and adequate remedy. The ancient Hebrews, bitten by fiery serpents, were not to mix up medicines of their own invention to help out the cure. It was all-sufficient for them to look up to the remedy that God had provided. God wanted them to understand that the healing was altogether His own work. The serpent on a pole was the only external object connected with their cure; they were to look to this, and in this most simple way—only by an expecting look, indicative of simple faith—they were to receive their cure.

A Present Remedy

Christ is to be lifted up as a *present* remedy. So was the serpent. The cure that came about then was present, immediate. It involved no delay.

The Appointed Remedy

This bronze serpent was God's appointed remedy. Christ, too, is a remedy appointed by God, sent down from heaven for this specific purpose. It was indeed very wonderful that God appointed a bronze serpent for such a purpose—such a remedy for such a malady. It is no less wonderful that Christ was lifted up in agony and blood as a remedy for both the punishment for sin and the power of sin over the heart.

A "Divinely Certified" Remedy

The bronze serpent was a divinely certified remedy—not a human concoction with a high-sounding name, but a remedy prepared and brought forth by God Himself, under His own guarantee of its ample healing powers.

So was Christ. The Father testifies to the perfect adequacy of Jesus Christ as a remedy for sin. Jesus Christ must now be held up from the pulpit as one crucified for the sins of men. His great power to save lies in His atoning death.

He must not only be held up from the pulpit, but this exhibition of His person and work must also be endorsed, not contradicted, by the experience of those who behold Him.

Suppose that, in Moses' time, many who looked upon the bronze serpent were seen to be still dying. Who could have believed the declaration of God through Moses, that *"everyone who is bitten, when he looks at it, shall live"*? Undoubtedly, the Hebrews had many living witnesses who had been bitten and bore the scars of those wounds, but who had been healed by looking. Every such case confirmed the faith of the people in God's word and in His power to save. It is the same with the Gospel. Christ must be represented in His fullness, and this representation should be powerfully endorsed by the experience of His friends. Christ presents Himself as One ready and willing to save. Therefore, this is the thing to be shown.

This must be sustained by the testimony of His living witnesses.

The Look of Faith

As the first point of similarity is the lifting up of the object to be looked upon, the second is the looking itself.

Men looked upon the serpent, expecting divine power to heal them. Even those ancient men, in that comparatively dark age, understood that the serpent was only a type, not the cause of salvation in itself.

There is something very remarkable in the relationship of faith to healing. Take, for example, the case of the woman who had a flow of blood. She had heard something about Jesus and somehow had caught the idea that if she could only touch the hem of His garment, she would be made whole. (See Luke 8:43–48.) Imagine her pressing her way along through the crowd, faint with weakness, pale, and trembling. If you had seen her, you would perhaps have cried out, "What will this poor dying invalid do?"

She knew what she was trying to do. Unnoticed by all, she reached the spot where the Holy One stood. She put forth her feeble hand and touched His garment. Suddenly He turned around and asked, *"Who touched Me?"* (v. 45). The disciples, astonished at such a question under such circumstances, replied, *"Master, the multitudes throng and press You, and You say, 'Who touched Me?'"* (v. 45).

The fact was, somebody had touched Him with faith to be healed, and He knew that the healing power had gone forth from Himself to some believing heart. How beautiful an illustration this is of simple faith! And how wonderful the connection between the faith and the healing!

In the same way, the Hebrews received that wonderful healing power by simply looking toward the bronze serpent. No doubt this was a great mystery to them, yet it was no less a fact. Let them look; the looking brought the cure, although not one of them could tell how the healing power came. Likewise, we are to look to Christ, and in looking, to receive the healing power. It does not matter how little we understand the mode by which the looking gives us the remedy for sin.

Looking Away from Ourselves

This looking to Jesus implies that we look away from ourselves. There is to be no mixing up of counterfeit medicines with the great remedy. Such a course is always sure to fail. Thousands fail in just this way, forever trying to be healed partly by their own stupid, self-willed works, as well as partly by Jesus Christ. There must be no looking to man or to any of man's doings or man's help. All dependence must be on Christ alone. This is true not only in reference to pardon for sin, but also in reference to sanctification. Sanctification is accomplished by faith in Christ. It is only through faith that you get the divine influence—the Spirit of God—that sanctifies the soul; and this divine influence, in some of its manifestations, was the power that healed the Hebrews in the wilderness.

Looking to Christ implies looking away from ourselves in the sense of not relying at all on our own works for the cure desired, not even on works of faith. The looking is toward Christ alone as our all-prevalent, all-sufficient, and present Remedy.

There is a constant tendency in Christians to depend on their own doings, and not on simple faith in Christ. The woman who had the flow of blood seemed to have toiled many years to find relief before she came to Christ. No doubt she had tried everybody's prescriptions and had taxed her own ingenuity to its utmost capacity, but all was of no avail. At last she heard of Jesus. He was said to do many wonderful works. She said within herself, "This must be the promised Messiah, who was to bear our sicknesses and heal all the diseases of men. Oh, let me rush to Him, for if I may just touch the hem of His garment, I will be whole." She did not stop to philosophize upon the mode of the cure; she depended on no man's philosophy and had none of her own. She simply said, "I have heard of One who is mighty to save, and I will hurry to Him."

The same is true of being healed of our sins. Losing hope of all help in ourselves or in any other name than Christ's, and being assured that there is power in Him to work out the cure, we expect it of Him, and we go to Him in order to obtain it.

Several times within the last few years, people have come to me with the question, "Can I be saved from my sins—actually saved—so that I will not fall again into the same sins, and under the same temptations?" I have said, "Have you ever tried looking to Jesus?" They reply, "Yes." "But have you expected that you will be actually saved from sin by looking to Jesus, and will be filled with faith, love, and holiness?" "No, I did not expect that."

Now suppose someone had looked at the bronze serpent as a kind of experiment. He had no faith in what God said about being cured by looking, but he was inclined to try it. He looked a little and paid attention to his feelings, to see how it affected him. He did not believe God's word, but since he did not absolutely *know* whether it was true or false, he agreed to try it. This is not *looking* at all in the sense of our text. This would not have cured the bitten Israelite; it cannot heal the poor sinner. There is no faith in it. Sinners must look to Christ with both the desire and the intention of being saved. Salvation is the thing for which they look.

Suppose one had looked toward the bronze serpent, but with no willingness or intention to be cured. This would have done him no good. Nor can it do sinners any good to think of Christ except as a Savior, and a Savior for their own sins.

Finding a Remedy for All Sin

Sinners must look to Christ as a remedy for all sin. To wish to make some exception, sparing some sins but agreeing to abandon others, indicates pure rebellion of the heart. This approach can never move the All-seeing One. There cannot be honesty in the heart that seeks deliverance from sin only in part.

Looking to Christ Immediately

Sinners may look to Christ at once, without the least delay. They need not wait until they are almost dead under their illness. For the bitten Israelite, it was of no use to delay his looking to the serpent until he found himself in the jaws of death. He might have said, "I am clearly wounded, but I do not see much swelling yet; I do not feel the poison spreading through my system. I cannot look at the bronze serpent yet, for my case is not yet desperate enough. I could not hope to excite the pity of the Lord in my present condition; therefore, I must wait." There would have been no need for such delay in this case. Nor is there any need for it in the sinner's case now.

Looking for Blessings Promised

We must look to Christ for blessings promised—not to works, but to faith. It is interesting to see how many mistakes are made on this point. Many people think that there must be great mental agony, long periods of fasting, many bitter tears, and strong crying for mercy before deliverance can be looked for. They do not seem to know that all their displays of grief and distress can do no good, because such displays are not simple faith or any part of faith. Indeed, grief and distress are in no way needed in order to gain the sympathies of the Savior. Suppose, under the serpent-plague of the wilderness, men had concocted fake remedies, creating various gauzes, ointments, and purifiers of the blood. All this treatment could do no good, for there was only one effective cure: if a man were bitten and knew it, he needed only to look to the bronze serpent for his cure.

The case of the sinner is similar. If one is a sinner and knows it, he is prepared to come to Jesus. It will do him no good to go about getting counterfeit prescriptions or mixing up remedies of his own, when God has already provided the great Remedy. Yet many people have a constant tendency toward this very thing—toward relying on a variety of counterfeit spiritual remedies. See how the sinner toils and agonizes! He would circle heaven and earth to work out his own salvation, in his own way, to his own credit, by his own works. See how he worries himself in the multitude of his own plans! Before he arrives at simple faith, he finds himself in the deep mire of despair. "Alas," he cries, "there can be no hope for me! Oh, my soul is lost!"

But at last the gleam of light breaks through the thick darkness, and the sinner declares, "Possibly Jesus can help me! If He can, then I will live, but not otherwise, for surely there is no help for me but in Him." There he is in his despair—bowed down in weariness of soul and worn out with his vain attempts to help himself in other ways. Now the sinner looks for help from above. "There is nothing else I can do but cast myself utterly, in all my hopelessness, upon Jesus Christ. Will He receive me? Perhaps He will, and that is enough for me to know." The sinner thinks a little further, "Perhaps, yes, perhaps He will. No, more than that, I think He will, for they tell me He has done so for other sinners. I think He will—yes, I know He will—and here's my guilty heart! I will trust Him—yes, *'though He slay me, yet will I trust Him'* (Job 13:15)."

Have any of you experienced anything like this?

> Perhaps He will admit my plea,
> Perhaps will hear my prayer.

This is as far as the sinner can dare to go at first, but there is no need for any *perhaps.* Soon you hear him crying out, "Christ says He will; I must believe Him!" Then faith gets hold and rests on promised faithfulness, and, before he is aware, the sinner's soul is *"like the chariots of Amminadib"* (Song 6:12 KJV), and he finds his heart full of peace and joy as one on the borders of heaven.

REMARKS

1. When it is said in John 12, *"I, if I am lifted up from the earth, will draw all peoples to Myself,"* the language is indeed universal in form. However, it cannot be interpreted as strictly universal without being brought into conflict with biblical truth and known facts. This is only a common way of referring to a great multitude.

Thus, Christ may well have been saying, "I will draw great numbers—a vast multitude that no man can number." There is nothing here in the context or in the subject to require the strictly universal interpretation.

2. This usage of the bronze serpent was undoubtedly designed to try the faith of the Israelites. God often put their faith to the test, and often adapted His providences to educate their faith—to draw it out and develop it. He did the same thing in this situation. They had sinned. Therefore, fiery serpents had come among them, and many of the people were poisoned and dying on every side. God said, *"Make a fiery serpent, and set it on a pole; and it shall be that everyone who is bitten, when he looks at it, shall live."* This put their faith to the test.

3. It is certainly possible that many perished through mere unbelief, although the provisions for their salvation were most abundant. "We are expected to look at a serpent! How ridiculous!" they might have said scornfully. Perhaps some set themselves to philosophizing on the matter. "We," they may have said, "will much sooner trust our physicians than these old wives' tales. What philosophical connection can any man see between looking upon a piece of bronze and being healed of a serpent's bite?"

In a similar fashion, many people now discount the Gospel. They wonder how any healing power can come of gospel faith. True, they hear some people say they are healed—people who say they know the healing power has gone to their very souls, and who cry, "I looked to Jesus, and I was healed and made whole from that very hour." But they consider all this as mere fanatical delusion. They can see none of their philosophy in it.

But *is* this fanaticism? Is it any more strange than that a man bitten by a poisonous snake would be healed by obeying God's command and looking at a bronze serpent?

4. Many are hindered by the simplicity of the Gospel. They say they want something more intelligible! They want to see through it, and they will not trust what they cannot explain. But it is so simple that their philosophy cannot see through it. It is on this ground that many people stumble at the doctrine of sanctification by faith in Christ.

Yet the analogy provided by one of our texts is complete. Men are to look to Jesus so that they *"should not perish but have eternal life."* And who does not know that eternal life involves entire sanctification?

5. The natural man always seeks some way of salvation for which he can take the credit. He wants to work out some form of self-righteousness and does not know about trusting in Christ alone. It does not seem to him natural or philosophical.

6. There is an amazing and most alarming state of things in many churches: there is almost no Christ in their experience. It is obvious that He holds an exceedingly small space in their hearts. Far from knowing what salvation is as a thing to be attained by simply believing in Christ, they can only give you an experience similar to the one portrayed in the following dialogue:

Speaker 1: How did you become a Christian?
Speaker 2: I just made up my mind to serve the Lord.
Speaker 1: Is that all?
Speaker 2: That's all.
Speaker 1: Do you know what it is to receive eternal life by simply looking to Jesus?
Speaker 2: I don't think I understand that.
Speaker 1: Then you are not a Christian.

The Savior Lifted Up

Christianity, from beginning to end, is received from Christ by simple faith. In this way, and only in this way, does the pardon of sin come to the soul. Also, this is the only way in which one can receive the peace of God, passing all understanding, which lives in the soul along with faith and love. (See Philippians 4:7.) Thus, sanctification comes through faith in Christ.

What, then, shall we think of the religion that leaves Christ out of the picture? Many people are looking for some wonderful sign or token, not understanding that it is by faith that they are to be brought completely into affinity with Christ and into participation with His own life. By faith, Christ unites them to Himself. Faith working by love draws them into living union with His own moral being. All this is done when the mind simply looks to Christ in faith.

When the serpent was lifted up, no doubt many perished because they would not accept and act upon such a simple plan of remedy. Many perished because they did not and would not realize their danger. If they saw men cured, they would say, "We don't believe it was done by the bronze serpent on the pole. Those men were not much poisoned; they would not have died anyhow." Such people assume that those who ascribe their cure to the power of God are mistaken.

Many also perished from delay. They waited to see whether they were in danger of dying. And still they waited, until they were so crazed that they could only lie down and die.

Now, think of the sinner's case in regard to the Gospel. Some people are occupied with other matters that are more important just now, and of course they must delay their acceptance of the Savior. Many are influenced by others' opinions. They hear many stories; perhaps they hear of a man who looked and yet lost his life, or that another man did not look and yet was saved. People also have different opinions about their supposedly "Christian" neighbors, and this hinders many. They hear that some begin enthusiastic and zealous for religion, but seem to fail. They looked as they thought they should, but all in vain. Perhaps it was so, for these people might have looked without real faith. Some sinners will philosophize until they make themselves believe it is all a delusion to look to Christ. They think they see many people appearing to look who yet find no healing. Who can believe where there are so many stumbling blocks?

We may suppose that such discouragements drove some into despair in the wilderness, and certainly we see that the same causes produce these effects in the case of sinners today. Some people think they have committed the unpardonable sin. They group themselves among *"those who were once enlightened"* (Heb. 6:4), for whom *"there no longer remains a sacrifice for sins, but a certain fearful expectation of judgment, and fiery indignation"* (Heb. 10:26–27). Some are sure it is too late for them now. Their hearts are as hard as a millstone. All is dark and desolate as the grave. You may know of someone whose very look is that of a lost soul. Perhaps some of you are reasoning and disbelieving in this very way!

Many people may have neglected the bronze serpent because they thought they were getting better. They saw some change of symptoms. Sinners do the same thing. They feel better for going to church; indeed, there is so much improvement, they take it that they are undoubtedly doing well.

Many of the ancient Hebrews may have refused to look because they had no good hope, because they were full of doubts. If you had been there, you would have found a great variety of conflicting views, often even between brothers and sisters, fathers and mothers, parents and children. Some would ridicule those who believed; some would become angry; some wouldn't believe anyhow. Some sinners who ought to be seeking Christ are deterred by reasons fully as frivolous and foolish as these.

It is easy for us to see the analogy between the bronze serpent and Christ the Savior. I need not push the analogy any further. But the question for you now is this: Do you really believe that *"as Moses lifted up the serpent in the wilderness, even so must the Son of Man be lifted up, that whoever believes in Him should not perish but have eternal life"*? Do you understand the simple remedy of faith? Perhaps you ask, "What were they to believe?" They were to believe that, if they really looked at the bronze serpent on the pole, they would certainly experience the needed healing. It was God's certified remedy, and they were to regard it as such.

And what are you to believe now? That Christ is the great antitype of the serpent lifted up in the wilderness, and that you are to receive from Him by simple faith all the blessings of a full and free salvation. Yes, *by simple faith*. Do you understand this? You might say to these things, "What? May I, a sinner, just fix my eyes on Jesus in simple faith? Who may do this? Is it I? How can it be that I have this privilege?"

Some of you, for many months or years, have been trying to work yourselves into a certain state of mind. You are wishing intensely that you could feel such and such—according to some ideal you have in your minds. Don't you understand that you need to look by faith, and to let this look of faith be to you like the touch of the poor woman with the flow of blood was to her dying body? You need to believe that if you look to Christ in simple trust, He surely will receive you, will give you His divine love and peace and life and light, and will really make them pulsate through your whole moral being. Do you believe it? No, don't you see that you do *not* believe it? But you say, "It is a great mystery!" I am not going to explain it, nor will I presume that I can do so, any more than I can explain how that woman was healed by touching the hem of the Savior's garment. The touch and the looking were only the means by which the power was to be received. The manner in which God operates is a thing of small consequence to us; let us be satisfied that we know what we must do to secure the operations of His divine Spirit in *"all things that pertain to life and godliness"* (2 Pet. 1:3).

Undoubtedly, you have had confused ideas of the way of salvation, perhaps contriving and speculating, and working upon your own feelings. You pray, and having prayed, you say, "Now let me watch and see if this prayer has given me salvation!" Imagine if the Hebrew people, when bitten by serpents and commanded to look to the bronze serpent, had gone around applying an ointment here, using another drug there, all the time losing sight of the one thing that God told them would infallibly cure. Oh, why do men forget, and why do they not understand, that all good needed by us comes from God by simple faith? When we see any need, there is Christ, to be received by faith alone. His promises leave no need unmet.

Now, if this is the way of salvation, how astonishing that sinners look every other way but toward Christ, and put forth all other sorts of effort except the effort to look at once in simple faith to their Savior! How often we see them discouraged and confused, toiling so hard and so utterly in vain. No wonder they are so greatly misled! Go around among the churches and ask, "Did you ever *expect* to be saved from sin in this world?" People will say, "No, but I expect to be saved at death." Inasmuch as Christ has been quite unsuccessful in His efforts to sanctify your soul during your life, do you really think He will send death to help the work along?

Can you believe this?

While Christians disown the glorious doctrine of present sanctification by faith in Christ—accomplished for each man according to his faith—it cannot be expected that they will teach sinners how to look to Christ in simple faith for pardon. Knowing so little of the power of faith in their own experience, how can they teach others effectively, or even truthfully? Since the blind are leading the blind, it is no wonder that, in the end, both have fallen into the ditch. (See Matthew 15:14.)

There seems to be no remedy for such an end except for professing Christians to become *"the light of the world"* (Matt. 5:14) and to learn the meaning and know the experience of simple faith. Once faith has been learned, they will experience its transforming power and will be able to teach others the way of life.

Chapter 3

Where Sin Occurs, God Cannot Wisely Prevent It

*It is impossible that no offenses should come, but
woe to him through whom they do come!
—Luke 17:1*

An offense, as the term is used in this passage, is an occasion of falling into sin. It is anything that causes another to sin and fall.

It is plain that the offender in this passage is thought to be *voluntary* and *sinful* in his act; otherwise, the woe of God would not be proclaimed upon him. Consequently, the passage assumes that this sin is in some sense necessary and unavoidable. What is true of this sin in this respect is true of all other sin. Indeed, any sin may become an offense in the sense of being a temptation to others to sin; therefore, its inevitability would then be affirmed by this text.

The doctrine of this text, therefore, is that sin, under the government of God, cannot be prevented. In this chapter, I will examine this doctrine and show that sin is nevertheless utterly inexcusable. Then I will answer some possible objections and conclude with remarks.

Who Cannot Prevent Sin?

When I say it is impossible to prevent sin under the government of God, the statement still calls for another inquiry: Where does this impossibility lie? Is it on the part of the sinner, or on the part of God? Which is true—that the sinner cannot possibly help sinning, or that God cannot prevent his sinning?

The first supposition answers itself, for it could not be sin if it were utterly unavoidable. It might be the sinner's misfortune, but nothing could be more unjust than to attribute it to him as his crime.

But we will better understand where this impossibility lies if we first recall some of the elementary principles of God's government. Let us therefore consider that God's government over men is moral, and that it is known to be such by every intelligent being. By the term *moral,* I mean that it governs by influence, not by physical force. This government knows that man's mind can understand truth, can appreciate its role in man's happiness, can judge what is right by the conscience, and through the will can determine a course of voluntary action in view of God's claims. Thus, God governs the mind in a way that He does not govern matter. The planetary worlds are controlled by quite a different sort of power. God does not control them in their orbits by moral influences, but by a physical power.

I said that all men know this government to be moral by their own consciousness. When its precepts and penalties come before their minds, they are conscious that an appeal is being made to their voluntary powers. They are never conscious of any physical agency forcing obedience.

God's government implies that man has the power to will or not to will: man can will right or will wrong, can choose or refuse the great good that Jehovah promises. It also implies intelligence. The beings to whom law is addressed are capable of understanding it. They also have a conscience, as I have said, by which they can understand the significance of its obligations.

You need to distinguish between the influence of motives on the mind and of physical force upon matter. The former implies voluntariness; the latter does not. The former is adapted to the mind and has no adaptation to matter; the latter is adapted to matter, but has no possible application to the mind. In God's government over the human mind, everything is voluntary; nothing is coerced by physical force. Indeed, it is impossible for physical force to directly influence the mind. Where one is compelled to act, his powers of moral agency end.

If it were possible for God to force the will as He forces the moon along in its orbit, He would subvert the very idea of a moral government. Neither praise nor blame could be attached to any actions of beings who were moved to act in this way. The nature of persuasion is that it can be resisted. Thus, God's creatures must have power to resist any amount of even His persuasion. There can be no power in heaven or earth to coerce the will in the way that matter is coerced. The nature of the mind forbids its possibility. And if it were possible, it would still be true that if God were to coerce the human will, He would cease to govern morally.

God is infinitely wise. Men can no more doubt this truth than they can doubt their own existence. He has infinite knowledge. He knows everything—He knows all objects of knowledge, and knows them all perfectly. He is also infinitely good, His will being always conformed to His perfect knowledge and always controlled by His infinite benevolence.

His infinite goodness implies that He does the best He can, always and everywhere. In no instance does He ever fail to do the very best He can do. Thus, He can say to every creature, "What more can I do to prevent sin than I am doing?" Indeed, He appeals to every intelligent mind in this way. He made this appeal through Isaiah to the ancient Jews: *And now, O inhabitants of Jerusalem and men of Judah, judge, please, between Me and My vineyard. What more could have been done to My vineyard that I have not done in it?"* (Isa. 5:3–4).

Every moral agent in the universe knows that God has done the best He could do in regard to sin. Don't you know this, each one of you? Certainly you do. He Himself, in all His infinite wisdom, could not suggest a better course than the one He has taken. Men know this truth so well that they can never know it better. You may at some future time realize it more fully when you come to see its millions of illustrations drawn out before your eyes, but no demonstration can prove it more perfectly than it is proved to your own mind today.

Now, sin does, in fact, exist under God's government. For this sin, God is either to blame or not to blame. But everyone knows that God is not to blame for this sin, for man's own mind affirms that He would prevent it if He wisely could. If He were able to wisely prevent sin wherever it actually occurs, then not to do so certainly would nullify all our ideas of His goodness and wisdom. He would be the greatest sinner in the universe if, with power and wisdom adequate to prevent sin, He had failed to prevent it.

Here let me also note that what God cannot do wisely, He cannot morally do at all. For He cannot act unwisely. He cannot do things that wisdom forbids. To do so would be to undeify Himself. The supposition would make Him cease to be perfect, and this would be equivalent to ceasing to be God.

Suppose that God were to intervene unwisely to prevent a sinner from sinning. In such a case, He would sin Himself. I speak now of each instance in which God does not, in fact, intervene to prevent sin. Let us look at a case in which, if God were to intervene unwisely to prevent sin, He would prevent a man from sinning at the expense of sinning Himself.

The case is that of a sinner who is about to fall before temptation, or in more correct language, is about to rush into some new sin. God cannot wisely prevent his doing so. Now, what can be done? Will He let that sinner rush on to his chosen sin and self-made ruin; or will He step forward, unwisely, sin Himself, and incur all the frightful consequences of such a step? He lets the sinner bear his own responsibility. Why shouldn't He? Who could wish that God would sin? This explains every case in which man does in fact sin and God does not prevent it.

This is not speculation; no truth can be more irresistibly certain than this. I once heard a minister say in a sermon, "It is not irrational to suppose that in each case of sin, it occurs as it does because God cannot prevent it." After he came down from the pulpit, I said to him, "Why did you leave the matter that way? You left your hearers to suppose that there might be some other way; that this was only a possible theory, yet that some other theory was perhaps even more probable. Why did you not say, 'This theory is certain and must necessarily be true'?" Thus, the impossibility of preventing sin lies not in the sinner, but wholly with God.

Sin, it should be remembered, is nothing but an act of free will, always committed against one's convictions of what is right. Indeed, if a man did not know that selfishness is sin, it would not be sin in his case.

Sin is always committed against and in spite of motives of infinitely greater weight than those that lead one to sin. The very fact that man's conscience condemns the sin proves that, even in his own mind, the motives to sin are infinitely contemptible. Every sinner knows that sin is a willful abuse of his own powers as a moral agent—of the noblest powers of his being, for which he is said to be made in the image of God. (See Genesis 1:26.) Though he is made like God with these exalted attributes, though he is capable of determining his own voluntary activities intelligently if he will, still in every act of sin he abuses and degrades these powers, tramples down in the dust the image of God that is stamped on his being. With the capacities to become like an angel, he makes himself a fool. Clothed with a dignity of nature akin to that of his Maker, he chooses to debase himself to the level of savage beasts and of devils. With a face naturally looking upward, with a mind that grasps the great truths of God, with a reason that assumes and affirms the great principles involved in his moral duties, and with capacities that make him fit to sit on a nation's throne, he says, "Let me take this glorious image of God and debase it in the dust! Let me cast myself down, until there is no lower depth of degradation to which I can sink!"

Sin is, in every instance, a dishonoring of God. Every sinner must know this. It casts off His authority, spurns His advice, mistreats His love. Truly God Himself says, *"A son honors his father, and a servant his master. If then I am the Father, where is My honor? And if I am a Master, where is My reverence?"* (Mal. 1:6).

What sinner ever supposed that God neglects to do anything He wisely can do to prevent sin? If this is not true, what is conscience but a lie and a delusion? Conscience always affirms that God is clear of all guilt in reference to sin. In every instance in which conscience condemns the sinner, it fully acquits God.

Thus I have shown that sin, in every instance of its commission, is utterly inexcusable.

Objections Answered

Now I will present and answer some objections.

Q: If God is infinitely wise and good, why do we need to pray at all? If He will surely always do the best possible thing and all the good He can do, why do we need to pray?

A: Because His infinite goodness and wisdom demand it of us. Who could ask a better reason than this? If you believe in His infinite wisdom and goodness, if you make this belief the basis of your objection, and if you are honest, you will certainly be satisfied with this answer.

Also, it might be wise and good for Him to do many things asked of Him in prayer that He could not wisely do if unasked. You cannot, therefore, infer that prayer never changes the course that God voluntarily pursues.

Q: Why should we pray to God to prevent sin, if He cannot prevent it? If God cannot prevent sin under the circumstances in which sin exists, why go to Him and ask Him to prevent it?

A: We pray for the very purpose of changing the circumstances. This is our objective. And prayer does change the circumstances. If we step forward and offer *"effective, fervent prayer"* (James 5:16), this quite changes the state of the case. Think of Moses pleading with God to spare the nation after their great sin in the matter of the golden calf. God said to him, *"Let Me alone, that I may destroy them and blot out their name from under heaven; and I will make of you a nation mightier and greater than they"* (Deut. 9:14). "No," said Moses, "for what will the Egyptians say? And what will all the nations say? For a long time they have said, 'The God of that people will not be able to get them through that vast wilderness.' Therefore, what will You do for Your great name? *'Yet now, if You will forgive their sin; but if not, I pray, blot me out of Your book which You have written'* (Exod. 32:32)."

This prayer, coming up before God, greatly changed the circumstances of the case. Because of this prayer, God could honorably spare the nation—it was honorable for Him to answer this prayer.

Q: Why did God create moral agents at all if He foresaw that He could not prevent their sinning?

A: Because He saw that, on the whole, it was better to do so. In His omnipotence, He could prevent some sin in this race of moral agents; He could overrule what He could not wisely prevent, so as to bring out from it a great deal of good. Thus, in the long run, He saw it better, with all the results before Him, to create man as a moral agent rather than to hold back from doing so. Therefore, wisdom and love made it necessary for Him to create man as such. Having the power to create a race of moral beings—having also the power to convert and save a vast multitude of them, and power to overrule the sin He would not prevent so that it would bring about immense good—how could He not create man as He did?

Q: But if God cannot prevent sin, will He not be unhappy?

A: No; He is entirely satisfied to do the best He can and to accept the results.

Q: Is this not limiting the Holy One of Israel?

A: No. It is no limitation of God's power to say that He cannot do anything that is unwise. Nor do we limit His power when we say, "He cannot move the mind as

He moves a planet." That which is naturally absurd and impossible is not under anyone's power.

Q: Couldn't God prevent sin by annihilating each moral agent the instant before he would sin?

A: Undoubtedly He could, but we know that if this were wise, He would have done it. He has not done it, certainly not in all cases; therefore, it is not always wise.

Q: Then why doesn't God give more of His Holy Spirit?

A: He does give all He can wisely give, under existing circumstances. To suppose He might give more than He does, circumstances being the same, is to cast doubt on His wisdom or His goodness.

Some people seem greatly horrified at the idea of setting limits to God's power. Yet they make assumptions that inevitably cast doubt on His wisdom and His goodness. Such people need to consider that, if we must choose between limiting His power on the one hand, or His wisdom and His love on the other, it is infinitely more honorable to Him to adopt the former alternative than the latter. To strike a blow at His moral attributes is to annihilate His throne. Furthermore, as I have already suggested, you do not in any offensive sense limit God's power when you assume that He cannot do things that are naturally impossible and that He cannot act unwisely.

I pray that these remarks suffice in answer to the above objections.

REMARKS

1. We may see the only sense in which God could have intended the existence of sin. He does not intend to

prevent it in any case where it does actually occur. Yet He does not intend to cause moral agents to sin—for example, He did not cause Adam and Eve to sin in the Garden, or Judas to betray Christ. All He intended to do was to leave them with only a certain amount of restraint—as much as He could wisely impose—and then if they would sin, let them bear the responsibility. He left them to act freely and did not actively prevent their sinning. But He never uses means to make men sin. He only refrains from using unwise means to prevent their sinning. Thus, His agency in the existence of sin is only neutral.

2. The existence of sin does not prove that it is the necessary means of the greatest good. This point has been often argued in theological discussions. I do not intend to go into it at length here, but will only say that in all cases in which men sin, they might obey God instead of sinning. Now the question is, If they were to obey rather than sin, would not a greater good come about? We have these two reasons to answer this question in the affirmative: first, that obedience naturally tends to promote good and disobedience tends to promote evil; and second, that in all those cases, God earnestly and positively commands obedience. It is fair to presume that He would command what would secure the greatest good.

3. The human conscience always justifies God. This is an undeniable fact—a fact that is universally known. The proof of it can never be made stronger, for it stands recorded in each man's heart. There is no conflict between the human conscience and God. The fact is, conscience always condemns the sinner and justifies God. It could not affirm obligation without justifying God. The real controversy, therefore, is not between God and the conscience, but between God and the *heart*. In every instance in which sin exists, conscience condemns the sinner and justifies God.

Everywhere, throughout all time, the human conscience has stood up to condemn each sinner, to compel him to sign his own death warrant and acquit his Maker of all blame. These are the facts of human nature and life.

4. Conversion consists precisely in this: the heart's consent to these decisions of the conscience. The heart is to come over to the ground occupied by the conscience, and to thoroughly consent to it as right and true. For a long time, the conscience has been speaking; it has always maintained one doctrine that has long been resisted by the heart. Now, in conversion, the heart comes over and gives its full assent to the decisions of conscience—that God is right, and that sin and the sinner are utterly wrong.

And now, do any of you want to know how you may become a Christian? This is it. Let your heart justify God and condemn sin, just as your conscience does. Let your voluntary powers yield to the necessary affirmations of your reason and conscience. Then all will be peaceful within because all will be right.

But you say, "I am trying to do this!" Indeed, some of you are trying to *resist* it to your utmost. You settle down, as it were, with your whole weight while God would gladly draw you by His truth and Spirit. Yet you think you are really trying to yield your hearts to God. A strange delusion!

5. In the light of this subject, we can see the reason for a general Judgment. God intends to clear Himself from all accusation of wrong in the matter of sin before the entire moral universe. Strange facts have transpired in His universe, and strange insinuations have been made against His course of action. These matters must all be set right. He will take time enough to do this. He

will wait until all things are ready. Obviously He will not bring out His great Day of Trial until the deeds of earth have all been worked—until all the events of this wondrous drama have had their full development. Until then, He will not be ready to make a full exposé of all His doings. *Then* He can and will do it most triumphantly and gloriously.

The revelations of that Day will undoubtedly show why God did not intervene to prevent every sin in the universe. Then He will satisfy us as to the reasons He had for allowing Adam and Eve to sin and for leaving Judas to betray his Master. We know now that He is wise and good, but we do not know all the particular reasons for His permitting of sin. Then He will reveal those particular reasons, as far as it may be best and possible. No doubt He will then show that His reasons were so wise and good that He could not have done better.

6. Sin will then appear infinitely inexcusable and abominable. It will then be seen in its true relationship toward God and His intelligent creatures—unspeakably blameworthy and guilty.

Suppose a son has gone far away from the paths of obedience and virtue. He has had one of the best of fathers, but he would not hear his counsels. He had a wise and affectionate mother, but he sternly resisted all the appeals of her tenderness and tears. Despite the most watchful care of parents and friends, he went astray. As one madly bent on self-destruction, he pushed on, reckless of the sorrow and grief he brought upon those he should have honored and loved. At last the results of such a course stand revealed. The guilty youth finds himself ruined in body, in fortune, and in name. He has sunk far too low to retain even self-respect. Nothing remains for him but agonizing reflections on past foolishness and guilt. "Alas," he cries, "I have almost killed my father, and long ago I had quite broken my mother's heart. All that a son's foolishness and crime could do, I have done to bring their gray hairs down to the grave with sorrow. Having done so much to ruin my best friends, I have brought down a double ruin on my own head. No sinner but myself ever was more deserving of being doubly damned."

Thus truth flashes upon his soul, and thus his heart shrinks back and his conscience thunders condemnation. It will be the same with every sinner when all his sins against God will stand revealed before his eyes, and there will be nothing left for him but intense and complete self-condemnation.

7. God's omnipotence is no guarantee to any man that either he or any other sinner will be saved. I know the Universalist affirms this to be so. He will ask, "Doesn't the fact of God's omnipotence, seen in connection with His infinite love, prove that all men will be saved?" No! It does not prove that God will save one soul. With even more proof of God's perfect wisdom, love, and power, we still could not infer that He will save even one sinner. We might just as reasonably infer that He will send the whole race to hell. How can we know what His wisdom will determine? How can we infer what the requirements of His government might demand? In fact, the only ground we have for the belief that He will save any sinner is not at all our inference from His wisdom, love, and power, but is wholly based on His own declarations regarding this matter. Our knowledge is wholly from revelation. God has said so, and this is all we know about it.

Furthermore, in reply to the Universalist, God's omnipotence saves nobody. Salvation is not brought about by physical omnipotence. It is only by moral power that God saves, and this can save no man unless he agrees to be saved.

8. How bitter the reflections that sinners must have on their deathbeds, and how fearfully agonizing it must be for them when they pass behind the veil and see things in their true light! When you have seen a sinner dying in his sins, did you ever think what an awful thing it is for a sinner to die? You can see the lines of anguish on his face; you see the look of despair; you observe that he cannot bear to hear about the awful future. There he lies, and death pushes on his stern assault. The poor victim struggles in vain against his dreaded foe. He sinks and sinks; his pulse runs lower and lower. Look in his glassy eyes; notice that haggard brow. For a moment, he does not breathe. But suddenly he stares as though he is terribly alarmed, throws up his hands wildly, screams frightfully, sinks down, and is gone—to return no more!

Where is he now? Not beyond the scope of thought and reflection. He can see back into the world he has left. He can still *think*. Indeed, his misery is that he can do nothing but think! The prisoner said in his solitary cell, "I could bear torture, or I could endure toil; but oh, to have nothing to do but to *think!* To hear the voice of a friend no more—to say not a word—to do nothing from day to day and from year to year but to *think!* That is awful." This is true of the lost sinner. Who can measure the misery of incessant, self-agonizing thought?

Now, when your thoughts rush upon you uncomfortably and you feel that you will almost become deranged, you can find some drop of comfort for your fevered lips. For a few moments, at least, you can fall asleep, forget your sorrows, and find a temporary rest. But when you reach the world where the wicked find no rest—where there can be no sleep, where not one drop of water can reach you to cool your tongue (see Luke 16:19–26)—oh, how can your heart endure or your hands be strong in that fearful hour? (See Ezekiel 22:14.) God tried in vain to bless and save you. You fought Him and brought down upon your guilty head a terrifying damnation!

9. What infinite consolation will remain for God after He has closed up all the scenes of earth! He will have banished the wicked and taken home the righteous to His heart of love and peace. He will say, "I have done all that I wisely could to save the race of man. I made sacrifices cheerfully, sent my well-beloved Son gladly, waited as long as it seemed wise to wait. Now it only remains for Me to overrule all this pain and woe for the utmost good, and to rejoice in the bliss of the redeemed forevermore."

But there, in that world of misery, the guilty are lost. Their groans swell out and echo up the walls of their pit of woe. Such is the evidence that God is good and wise and will surely sustain His throne in equity and righteousness forever. This teaches most impressive lessons concerning the awful doom of sin. Let it stand and bear its testimony, to warn other beings against a course so guilty and a doom so dreadful!

Among the doomed may be some of our own children. But God is just, and His throne unstained by their blood. The fact that they pull down such damnation on their heads will not mar the eternal joy of His kingdom. They insisted they would take the responsibility, and now they have it.

Sinner, do you not care for this today? Will you continue to treat the matter of your salvation lightly? I can tell you where you will take everything very seriously. When the great bell of time tolls the death knell of earth and calls her millions of sons and daughters to the Final Judgment, you will not be in a mood to take anything lightly! You will surely be there! It will be a time for serious thought—an awful time of dread. Are you ready to face its revelations and decisions?

Or do you say, "Enough, enough! I have withstood His grace and spurned His love long enough; I will now give my heart to God, to be His only, forevermore"?

Chapter 4

Quenching the Spirit

Do not quench the Spirit.
—1 Thessalonians 5:19

We hear a great deal about "not quenching the Spirit," but do we really understand what is meant by this Scripture? In this chapter, I will discuss the subject of quenching the Spirit, and I will show the following: How the Holy Spirit influences the mind, what can be inferred from the way the Spirit operates, what it is to quench the Spirit, how this may be done, and the consequences of quenching the Spirit.

How the Holy Spirit Influences the Mind

First, how does the Holy Spirit influence the human mind? I answer, not by the intervention of direct physical power. The action of the will is not influenced in this way, and it cannot be. The very supposition is absurd. That physical power could produce voluntary mental phenomena just as it does physical phenomena is both absurd and opposed to the idea of free agency. That the same physical power that moves a planet could move the human will is absurd.

Furthermore, the Bible informs us that the Spirit influences the human mind by means of truth. The Spirit persuades men to act in view of truth, as we ourselves influence our fellowmen by presenting truth to them. I do not mean that God presents truth to the mind in the same manner as we do. Of course, His method of doing it must differ from ours. We use the pen, our lips, or a gesture; we use the language of words. God does not use these means, yet still He reaches the mind with truth. Sometimes His providence suggests it, and then His Spirit brings it home to the heart with great power. Sometimes the Lord makes use of preaching; indeed, His ways are various. But whatever the method, the purpose is always the same; namely, to produce voluntary action in conformity to His law.

Now, if the Bible were entirely silent on this subject, we would still know, from the nature of our minds and from the nature of the influences that can move the human mind, that the Spirit exerts moral, not physical, influences on the mind. In this we are not left with a mere theory; rather, the Bible plainly testifies to the fact that the Spirit employs truth in converting and sanctifying men.

Inferences from the Way the Spirit Operates

Second, what is implied in this fact, and what must be inferred from it? God is physically omnipotent, and yet His moral influences exerted by the Spirit may be resisted. You will readily see that if the Spirit moved men by physical omnipotence, no mortal could possibly resist His influence. The Spirit's power would, of course, be irresistible—for who could withstand omnipotence? But we know that men can resist the Holy Spirit; for the nature of moral agency implies this, and the Bible asserts it.

The nature of moral agency implies that a person can yield to an influence if he so desires; he can choose whether or not to follow light. Where this power does not exist, moral agency cannot exist; and at whatever point this power ceases, there moral agency ceases also.

Hence, if our actions are to be those of moral agents, our moral freedom to do or not do must remain. It cannot be set aside or in any way overruled. If God were in any way to set aside our voluntary agency, He would at once be terminating our moral and responsible action. Suppose God were to take hold of a man's arm with physical omnipotence and forcibly use it in deeds of murder or of arson. Who does not see that the moral, responsible agency of that man would be entirely superseded? Yet this would no more supersede his moral agency than if God were to seize the man's will and compel it to act as He desired.

The idea that moral influence cannot be resisted originates in a misunderstanding as to the nature of the will and of moral action. The will of man can do nothing but act freely in view of truth and the motives that truth presents. To increase the amount of such influence will never impair the freedom of the will. No matter how vividly truth is perceived, or no matter how much the mind is influenced by truth, the will has the same changeless power to yield or not yield—to act or refuse to act in accordance with this revealed truth.

Force and moral agency are terms of opposite meaning. They cannot coexist. The one essentially rules out the other. Thus, to say that God, who is physically omnipotent, can and will force a moral agent in his moral action is to talk pure nonsense.

This fact shows not only that man can resist any work of God carried on by moral and not by physical power, but also that man may be in very great danger of resisting it. If the Lord carries the work forward by means of revealed truth, there may be imminent danger that men will neglect to study and understand this truth, or that, knowing it, they will refuse to obey it. Surely it is within the power of every man to shut out this truth from his thoughts and to bar his heart against its influence.

What Is Quenching the Spirit?

Third, we next inquire what it is to quench the Spirit. We readily understand the meaning of this when we come to see distinctly what the work of the Spirit is. His work is to enlighten the mind with the truth about God, ourselves, and our duty. For example, the Spirit enlightens the mind with the meaning of the Bible and its application to one's life. He takes the things of Christ and shows them to us. (See John 16:15.)

Now, there is such a thing as refusing to receive this light. You can shut your eyes against it. You have the power to turn your eyes entirely away and scarcely see it at all. You can utterly refuse to follow it even when you do see it, and in this case God ceases to present the truth to you.

Almost everyone knows by personal experience that the Spirit has the power to shed a marvelous light upon revealed truth, so that this truth stands before the mind in a new and most impressive form, and operates upon it with astonishing energy. But this light of the Spirit may be quenched.

There is a sort of heat, a warmth and vitality, so to speak, accompanying the truth when it is urged by the Spirit. For this reason, we say that a man's soul is warm if he has the Spirit of God, but that his heart is cold if he does not have the Spirit.

This vital heat produced by the Divine Spirit may be quenched. When a man resists the Spirit, he will certainly quench this vital energy that He exerts upon the heart.

How the Spirit May Be Quenched

Fourth, let us look at some of the ways in which the Spirit may be quenched.

Resisting the Truth

Men often quench the Spirit by directly resisting the truth that He presents to their minds. Sometimes men deliberately set themselves to resist the truth, determined that they will not yield to its power, at least for the present. In such cases, it is astounding to see how great the influence of the will is in resisting the truth. Indeed, the will can always resist any moral considerations, for, as we have seen, there is no such thing as forcing the will to yield to truth.

In cases in which the truth presses strongly on the mind, there is reasonable evidence that the Spirit is present by His power. And it is in precisely these cases that men are especially prone to set themselves against the truth, and thus are in the utmost peril of quenching the Spirit. They hate the truth presented—it crosses their chosen path of indulgence—they feel vexed and harassed by its claims; they resist and quench the Spirit of the Lord.

You have undoubtedly seen many such cases, and if so, you have certainly noticed another remarkable fact of usual occurrence—that after a short struggle in resisting truth, the conflict is over, and the particular truth almost utterly ceases to affect the mind. Individuals become hardened to its power; they seem quite able to overlook it and thrust it from their thoughts. They felt greatly annoyed by that truth until they had quenched the Spirit; now they are annoyed by it no longer.

If you have seen cases of this sort, you have undoubtedly seen how, as the truth pressed upon their minds, they became fidgety, sensitive, then perhaps angry, but still stubborn in resisting, until at length the conflict subsided. Then the truth made no more impression and became quite dead to them. They understood that truth only with the greatest dimness, and they cared nothing about it.

Haven't some of you had this very experience? Have you not resisted some truth until it has ceased to affect your minds? If so, then you may conclude that, in that case, you quenched the Spirit of God.

Supporting Error

The Spirit is often quenched by the attempt to support error. Men are sometimes foolish enough to attempt by argument to support a position that they have good reason to know is a false one. They argue it until they become committed to it; they indulge in a dishonest state of mind. Thus, they quench the Spirit and are usually left to believe the lie that they so unwisely attempted to advocate. I have seen many cases in which people began to defend a position known to be false, and they kept on until they quenched the Spirit of God—they believed their own lie, and, it is to be feared, will die under its delusions.

Judging Others without Love

Perhaps nothing more certainly quenches the Spirit than to condemn the motives of others and judge them

without a spirit of love. It is so unlike God, and so hostile
to the law of love; no wonder the Spirit of God is utterly
against it and turns away from those who indulge in it.

Using Harsh and Abusive Language

The Spirit is grieved by harsh and abusive language.
How often people grieve the Spirit of God by using such
language toward those who differ from them. It is always
safe to presume that people who indulge in such language have already grieved away the Spirit of God.

Displaying a Bad Temper

The Spirit of God is quenched by a bad temper.
When a bad temper and spirit are stirred up in individuals or in a community, a revival of religion can cease suddenly; the Spirit of God is put down and quenched. There
is no more prevailing prayer, and no more sinners are
converted.

Diverting Attention from the Truth

Often the Spirit is quenched by the diverting of the
attention from the truth. Since the Spirit operates
through the truth, it is obvious that we must pay attention to this truth that the Spirit desires to keep before
our minds. If we refuse to pay attention—we can refuse if
we choose to do so—we will almost certainly quench the
Holy Spirit.

Getting Carried Away

We often quench the Spirit by getting carried away
on any subject. If the subject is inconsistent with practical, divine truth, strong excitement diverts our attention
from the truth and makes it almost impossible for us to
feel its power. While the mind feels zealous concerning

the subject about which it is excited, it feels cold about the vital things of salvation. Hence, the Spirit is quenched.

It may surprise some people that the immoderate excitement may be on some religious topic. Sometimes I have seen a real tornado of feeling in a revival. But in such cases, truth loses its hold on the minds of the people; they are much too excited to have proper views of the truth and of the moral duties it teaches.

Not all religious excitement, however, is to be condemned—by no means. There must be enough excitement to rouse the mind to serious thought—enough to give the truth edge and power. But it is always well to avoid the measure of excitement that throws the mind from its balance and renders its perceptions of truth obscure or capricious.

Indulging Prejudice

The Spirit is quenched by indulging prejudicial thoughts and ideas. Whenever the mind is made up on any subject before it is thoroughly examined, that mind is shut against the truth, and the Spirit is quenched. When there is great prejudice, it seems impossible for the Spirit to act, and of course His influence is quenched. The mind is so committed that it resists the first efforts of the Spirit. Thousands have done this and have ruined their souls for eternity.

Therefore, everyone must keep his mind open to conviction and be sure to examine carefully all important questions, especially all those questions involving duty to God and man.

I am not saying that you should not be firm in maintaining your position after you thoroughly understand it and are sure it is the truth. But while pursuing your investigations, be sure you are really candid and yield your mind to all the reasonable evidence you can find.

Violating Conscience

The Spirit is often quenched by violating one's conscience. Under some circumstances, the violation of conscience seems to quench the light of God in the soul forever. Perhaps you have seen cases of this sort—where someone has had a very tender conscience on some subject, but all at once he appears to have no conscience at all on that subject. Of course, a change in conduct sometimes results from a change of views without any violation of conscience. But the case I speak of is where the conscience seems to have been killed. All that remains of it seems hard as a stone.

I have sometimes thought the Spirit of God has much more to do with conscience than we usually suppose. It is undeniable that men sometimes experience very great and sudden changes in the sensitivity of conscience that they feel on some subjects. How is this to be accounted for? Only by the assumption that the Spirit has power to rouse the conscience and make it pierce like an arrow. Then, when a man sins despite the disapproval of his conscience, the Spirit is quenched; the conscience loses all its sensitivity. An entire change takes place, and the man goes on to sin as if he never had any conscience to forbid it.

Sometimes the mind is awakened just on the brink of committing some particular sin. Perhaps something seems to say to him, "If you do this, you will be forsaken by God." A strange premonition forewarns him not to continue. Now, if he goes on, his whole mind receives a dreadful shock; his moral perceptions are strangely deranged and dimmed. A fatal violence is done to the conscience on that particular subject, at least, and indeed the injury to the conscience seems to affect all departments of moral action. In such circumstances, the Spirit of God seems to turn away and say, "I can do no more for you; I have warned you faithfully and can warn you no more."

All these results sometimes come about from neglect of plainly revealed duty. People shrink from known duty because they fear the opinions of others, or because they dislike some self-denial. In this trial, the Spirit does not leave them in a state of doubt as to their duty, but He keeps the truth and the claims of God vividly before their minds. Then, if an individual goes on and commits the sin despite the Spirit's warnings, his soul is left in awful darkness—the light of the Spirit of God is quenched perhaps forever.

I have seen many cases in which people are in great agony and even despair because they had evidently quenched the Spirit in the manner just described. Consider the case of a young man who underwent significant trial over the question of preparing himself for the ministry. He weighed the question for a long time, the claims of God being clearly set before him; but at last he resisted the convictions of duty, he went off and got married, and he turned away from the work to which God seemed to call him. Then the Spirit left him. For a few years, he remained entirely hardened as to what he had done and as to any claims of God upon him, but his wife eventually became ill and died. Then his eyes were opened; he saw what he had done.

He sought the Lord, but sought in vain. No light returned to his darkened, desolate soul. It no longer seemed his duty to prepare for the ministry; that call of God had ceased. His cup of wretchedness seemed to be filled to the brim. Often he spent whole nights in the most intense agony, groaning, crying for mercy, or musing in anguish upon the dire despair that spread its universe of desolation all around him. I have often feared he would take his own life, so perfectly wretched was he under these reproaches of a guilty conscience and these thoughts of deep despair.

I might mention many other similar cases. Men refuse to do what they know is their duty, and this refusal does fatal violence to their own moral sense and to the Spirit of the Lord. Consequently, there remains for them only *"a certain fearful expectation of judgment, and fiery indignation"* (Heb. 10:27).

Indulging Fleshly Appetites

People often quench the Spirit by indulging their appetites and passions. You would be astonished if you knew how often the Spirit is grieved by this means. Some people indulge their appetite for food to the injury of their health. Though they know they are injuring themselves, and though the Spirit of God urges and presses them to cease from ruinous self-indulgence, they persist in their course. Thus, they are given up by God, and henceforth their appetites control them, to the ruin of their spirituality and of their souls. The same may be said of any form of fleshly indulgence.

Indulging in Dishonesty

The Spirit is often quenched by indulging in dishonesty. Some businessmen will take little advantages in buying and selling, even when they are powerfully convinced of the great selfishness of this and when they see that this is by no means loving their neighbor as themselves. Suppose a man is about to drive a good bargain.

He may ask himself the question, "Is this right?" He may weigh the question for a long time and may say, "This neighbor of mine needs this item very much, and he will suffer if he does not get it. I could very well increase the price, but would this be doing to others as I want them to do to me?" The man thinks; he sees his duty, but he finally decides in favor of his selfishness. Eternity alone will disclose the consequences of such a decision.

When the Spirit of God has followed such individuals a long time, when He has made them see their danger, when He has kept the truth before them and even His last effort is ineffective, then the die is cast. After this, all restraints are gone, and the selfish man, abandoned by God, becomes worse and worse. Perhaps he will end up in prison, but certainly he will end up in hell!

Casting Off a Prayerful Spirit

Often men quench the Spirit by casting off prayer. Indeed, the Spirit must always be quenched when prayer is withheld. It is wonderful to see how naturally and earnestly the Spirit leads us to pray. If we were really led by the Spirit, we would be drawn many times a day to secret prayer, and we would be continually lifting up our hearts in silent shouts of praise whenever the mind is not focused on other pressing matters. The Spirit in the hearts of saints is preeminently a Spirit of prayer, and of course to restrain prayer must always quench the Spirit.

Perhaps some of you have been in this situation. You once had the spirit of prayer, but now you have none of it; you once had access to God, but now you have it no longer; you have no more enjoyment in prayer, no groaning and agonizing over the state of the church and of sinners. And if this spirit of prayer is gone, where are you now? Alas, you have quenched the Spirit of God—you have put out His light and repelled His influence from your soul.

Idle Conversation

The Spirit is quenched by idle conversation. Few seem to be aware how wicked this is and how certainly it quenches the Holy Spirit. Christ said, *"For every idle word men may speak, they will give account of it in the day of judgment"* (Matt. 12:36).

Various Spirits

Men quench the Holy Spirit by a spirit of frivolity and trifling, by indulging an irritable and fractious spirit, or by a spirit of laziness. Many indulge in this to such an extent that they altogether drive away the Holy Spirit.

Men also quench the Spirit by a spirit of procrastination, and by indulging themselves in making excuses for their neglect of duty. This is a sure way to quench the Spirit of God in the soul.

Resisting Sanctification

It is to be feared that many have quenched the Spirit by resisting the doctrine and duty of sanctification. For many years, this subject has been extensively discussed, and the doctrine has also been extensively opposed. Several ecclesiastical bodies have taken a stand against it, and sometimes members of these bodies have said and done things in their meetings that they would not by any means have said or done in their own prayer closets or pulpits. Is it not also probable that many ministers and some laymen have been influenced by this very ecclesiastical action to oppose the doctrine—the fear of man thus becoming a snare to their souls? (See Proverbs 29:25.)

May it not also be the case that some have opposed the doctrine because it raises a higher standard of personal holiness than they like—too high, perhaps, to permit them to hope as Christians, too high for their experience, and too high to suit their tastes and habits? Now who does not see that opposition to the doctrine and duty of sanctification on such grounds must certainly and fatally quench the Holy Spirit? No work lies nearer the heart of Jesus than the sanctification of His people. Hence, it greatly grieves Him to see this work hindered—much more to see it opposed and brought to nothing.

These considerations become very solemn when you contemplate the prevalent state of piety in many churches today. You need not ask, "Are Christians prayerful, self-denying, alive in faith, and full of love for God and man?" You need not ask if the work of sanctifying the church is moving on swiftly and manifesting itself by abounding fruits of righteousness; the answer meets you before you can even frame the question.

How unfortunate that the Spirit should be quenched under the diffusion of the very truth that ought to sanctify the church! What can save if the gospel promise, in all its fullness, is so perverted or resisted that, inevitably, the Spirit is quenched and the heart is hardened?

The Consequences of Quenching the Spirit

Fifth, let us examine the consequences of quenching the Holy Spirit.

Great Darkness of the Mind

Abandoned by God, the mind sees truth so dimly that truth makes no useful impression. Such individuals read the Bible without interest or profit. It becomes to them a dead letter, and they generally lay it aside unless some conflict leads them to search it. They take no spiritual interest in it that would make its perusal delightful.

Haven't some of you been in this state of mind? This is the darkness of nature that is common to men, when the Spirit of God is withdrawn.

Coldness toward Religion in General

Another result is that one develops great coldness toward religion in general. The mind does not have even part of the interest in spiritual things that men have in worldly things.

People often get into such a state that they are greatly interested in some worldly matters, but not in spiritual religion. Their souls are all awake while worldly things are the subject, but as soon as you suggest some spiritual subject, their interest is gone. You can scarcely get them to attend a prayer meeting. Surely they are in a worldly state of mind, for if the Spirit of the Lord was with them, they would be more deeply interested in religious services than in anything else.

You can see that their souls are all on fire for some political meeting or a play at the theater. But if you tell them of a prayer meeting or a revival meeting, they will not attend; or if they do, they feel no interest in the meeting's purpose.

Such individuals often seem not to know themselves. Perhaps they think they attend to these worldly things only for the glory of God; I will believe this when I see them interested in spiritual things as much.

When a man has quenched the Spirit of God, his religion is all outside. His vital, heart-affecting interest in spiritual things is gone.

It is indeed true that a spiritual man will take some interest in worldly things because he regards them as a part of his duty to God, and to him they are spiritual things.

Erroneous Religious Views Develop

When the Spirit is quenched, the mind falls very naturally into various errors in religion. The heart wanders from God and loses its hold on the truth; perhaps the person insists that he or she now holds a much more liberal and enlightened view of the subject than before.

A short time ago, I had a conversation with a man who had given up the idea that the Old Testament was inspired. He had also given up the doctrine of the Atonement, and indeed every distinctive doctrine of the Bible. He said to me, "I used to think as you do, but I have now come to take a more liberal and enlightened view of the subject." Indeed! A more liberal and enlightened view! He is so blinded that he does not see that Christ sanctioned the Old Testament as the oracles of God (see, for example, Matthew 21:42; 26:52–54), and yet he flatters himself that he now takes a more liberal and enlightened view! There can be nothing stronger than Christ's affirmations regarding the inspiration of the Old Testament, yet this man acknowledges these affirmations to be true while denying the very thing they affirm! A liberal and enlightened view—what nonsense!

How can you possibly account for such views except on the ground that, for some reason, the man has fallen into a strange, unnatural state of mind—a sort of stupidity in which moral truths have become clouded or distorted?

Everybody knows that there cannot be a greater absurdity than to admit the divine authority of the teachings of Christ and yet reject the Old Testament. The language of Christ affirms and implies the authority of the Old Testament. Certainly the Old Testament does not exhaust divine revelation; it left more things to be revealed. Christ taught much, but nothing more clearly than the divine authority of the Old Testament.

Unbelief

Quenching the Spirit often results in unbelief. What can account for such a case as the one I have just mentioned, unless it is this—that God has left the mind to fall into very great darkness?

Hardness of Heart

Another result is great hardness of heart. The mind becomes callous to all the truths that make it yielding and tender. The moral hardness of the heart determines how much it will be affected by truth. If the heart is very hard, truth makes no impression; if soft, then it is as yielding as air, and it moves quickly to the touch of truth from any direction.

Delusion as to One's Spiritual State

Another result of quenching the Spirit is deep delusion in regard to one's spiritual state. How remarkable that people will claim to be Christians when they have rejected every distinctive doctrine of Christianity! Indeed, such individuals sometimes claim that by rejecting almost the whole Bible, and its great plan of salvation by an atonement, they have become real Christians and have the true light. What utter foolishness!

How can such a delusion be accounted for except on the ground that the Spirit of God has abandoned such men to their own ways and left them to complete and perfect delusion?

Attempts to Justify Oneself in Wrongdoing

People in this state often justify themselves in most obvious wrongdoing, because they substitute *"darkness for light, and light for darkness"* (Isa. 5:20). They entrench themselves in perfectly false principles, as if those principles were true and could amply justify their misdeeds.

REMARKS

1. People often are not aware of what is going on in their minds when they are quenching the Spirit of God. Duty is presented and pressed upon them, but they do not realize that this is really the work of the Spirit of God. They are not aware of the present voice of the Lord to their hearts, nor do they see that this solemn impression of the truth is nothing other than the effect of the Holy Spirit on their minds.

2. So, when they come to hold different views and to abandon their former opinions, they seem to be unaware of the fact that God has departed from them. They flatter themselves that they have become very liberal and very much enlightened, and have only given up their former errors. But they do not see that the light they now walk in is darkness—all sheer darkness! *"Woe to those who... put darkness for light, and light for darkness"* (Isa. 5:20).

You now see how to account for the spiritual state of some people, so that you will not be misled. In the case I described above, suppose that I had taken it for granted that this man was truly taking a more rational and liberal view; I would have been misguided entirely.

3. I have good reason to know how individuals become Unitarians and Universalists, having seen at least several hundreds of instances. It is not by becoming more and more men of prayer and real spirituality, or by getting nearer and nearer to God. No, these people do not go on progressing in holiness, prayer, and communion with God, until in their high attainments they reach a point where they deny the inspiration of the Bible and give up public prayer, the ordinances of the Gospel, and probably secret prayer along with the rest. Those who give up these things are not led away while wrestling in prayer or while walking humbly and closely with God; no man ever got away from orthodox views while in this state of mind. Rather, men first get away from God and quench His Spirit; then they embrace one error after another; truth falls out of their minds (I might almost say that they lose the moral attributes that enable the mind to discern and understand the truth); and then darkness becomes so universal and so deceptive that men suppose themselves to be wholly in the light.

4. Such a state of mind is most deplorable and often hopeless. What can be done when a man has grieved the Spirit of God away?

5. When an individual or a community of people have quenched the Spirit, they are in the utmost danger of being given up to some delusion that will bring them quickly to destruction.

6. Those who insist that a religious movement cannot be resisted if it is the work of God take an entirely false stand. I have often seen cases where people would stop a revival and then say, "It was not a real revival, for if it had been it would not have stopped."

When a man adopts the opinion that he cannot stop the work of God in his own soul, nothing can be more perilous. When people adopt the idea that revivals come and go only by the agency of God, and not because of anything they might do, it will bring perfect ruin on them. There never was a revival that could exist three days under such a delusion. The solemn truth is that the Spirit is easily quenched. There is no moral work of His that cannot be resisted.

7. An immense responsibility pertains to revivals. There is always fearful danger that the Spirit will be resisted. It is the same when the Spirit is with an individual: there is the greatest danger that something will be said that is ruinous to his soul.

Many people—including some of you, my readers—are in the greatest danger. The Spirit often labors with sinners, and many have grieved Him away.

8. Many people do not seem to realize the nature of the Spirit's operations, the possibility of resisting Him, and the great danger of quenching the light of God in the soul.

I can think of many young people who were once thoughtful, but are now stupid. Is this not the case with you, young man, or with you, young woman? Have you not quenched the Spirit until your mind is darkened and your heart woefully hardened? How long before the death knell will toll over you and your soul will go down to hell? How long before you will lose your hold on all truth and the Spirit will have left you utterly?

But let me bring this appeal home to the hearts of those who have not yet utterly quenched the light of God in the soul. Do you find that truth still takes hold of your conscience, that God's Word flashes on your mind, that heaven's light is not yet utterly extinguished, and there is still a quivering of conscience? You hear that someone has died suddenly, and trembling seizes your soul, for you know that *you* may be singled out by the next blow. Then by all the mercies of God, I beg you to take care what you do. Do not quench the Holy Spirit, lest your sun go down in everlasting darkness. Just as you may have seen the sun set when it dipped into a dark, terrific, portentous thundercloud, so a sinner dies when he is overtaken by darkness!

Have you ever seen such a death? Dying, he seems to sink into an awful cloud of fire and storm and darkness. The scene is fearful, like a sunset of storms, of gathering clouds, of rolling thunders, and forked lightnings. The clouds gather low in the west; the spirit of storm rides on the gusts of wind; belching thunders seem as if they will divide the solid earth; the sun drops behind such a fearful cloud, and all is darkness! Similarly, I have seen a sinner give up the ghost and drop into a world of storms, howling tempests, and flashing fire.

Oh, how unlike the setting sun of a mild summer evening, when all of nature seems to put on her sweetest smile as she bids the king of day adieu! This is how those who believe in God die—without storm, without tempest. There may be paleness on the man's lip and a cold sweat on his brow, but there is beauty in his eye and glory in the soul. I knew of one woman, just converted, who was taken sick and brought down to the gates of death, yet her soul was full of heaven. Her voice was the music of angels; her countenance shone; her eyes sparkled as if the forms of heavenly glory were embodied in her dying features. When at last the moment of death arrived, she stretched out her dying hands and hailed the waiting multitude of spirits. "Glory to God!" she cried; "I am coming! I am coming!" Notice that she did not say "I am going," but "I am coming!"

But in comparison, look at the dying sinner. A frightful glare is on his face, as if he saw ten thousand demons!

He looks as if the setting sun were going down into an ocean of storms, to be lost in a world charged with tornadoes, storms, and death!

Young man or woman, you will die exactly the same way if you quench the Spirit of God. Jesus Himself has said, *"If you do not believe,...you will die in your sins"* (John 8:24). Beyond such a death, there is an awful hell.

Chapter 5

The Spirit Not Always Striving

❖

*And the LORD said, "My Spirit
shall not strive with man forever."
—Genesis 6:3*

In this chapter, we will take a close look at this verse
of Scripture from Genesis. In doing so, I will attempt
to answer the following questions: What is implied in
the assertion, *"My Spirit shall not strive with man forever"*? What is not intended by the Spirit's striving?
What is intended by it? How may it be known when the
Spirit strives with an individual? What is intended by His
not striving forever? Why will He not always strive?
What are some of the consequences of His ceasing to
strive with men?

Implications of the Assertion, "My Spirit
Will Not Always Strive"

First, what is implied in the assertion, *"My Spirit
shall not strive with man forever"*? One implication is
that the Spirit does *sometimes* strive with men. It is nonsense to affirm that He will not *always* strive if He does
not strive at least sometimes. Beyond all question, the

text assumes that God, by His Spirit, does strive sometimes with sinning men.

It is also implied that men resist the Spirit, for there
can be no strife unless there is also resistance. If sinners
always yielded at once to the teachings and guidance of
the Spirit, there would be no striving on the part of the
Spirit—in the sense that is implied here—and it would be
altogether improper to use the language that is used here.
In fact, the language of our text verse implies long-
continued resistance—so long-continued that God declares
that the struggle will not be kept up on His part forever.

I am well aware that sinners are prone to think that
they do not resist God. They often think that they really
want the Spirit of God to be with them and to strive with
them. Think of this! If a sinner really wanted the Spirit
of God to convert or to lead him, how could he resist the
Spirit? But, in fact, he does resist the Spirit. What Stephen affirmed of the Jews of his time is true of all sinners: *"You always resist the Holy Spirit"* (Acts 7:51). For
if there were no resistance on the sinner's part, there
would be no striving on the part of the Spirit. Therefore,
it is a mere absurdity to say that a sinner in a state of
mind to resist the Spirit can yet sincerely desire to be led
into truth and duty by the Spirit. But sinners are sometimes so deceived about themselves as to suppose that
they want God to strive with them, while really they are
resisting all He is doing, and are ready to resist all He
will do. Indeed, sinners are blinded to their own true
characters.

What the Spirit's Striving Is Not

Second, what is not intended by the Spirit's striving?
Here the main thing to be observed is that it is not any

form of physical struggling or effort whatsoever. It is not any force applied to our bodies. It does not attempt to push us literally along toward God or heaven. This is not to be thought of at all.

What the Spirit's Striving Is

What, then, is the striving of the Spirit? I answer, it is an energy of God, applied to the mind of man, setting truth before his mind, debating, reasoning, convincing, and persuading. The sinner resists God's claims, argues against them; then God, by His Spirit, meets the sinner and debates with him, just as two men might debate and argue with each other. The Holy Spirit, however, does not do this with a voice audible to the human ear, but He speaks to the mind and to the heart. The inner ear of the soul can hear His whispers.

Our Savior taught that when the Comforter came, He would *"reprove the world of sin, and of righteousness, and of judgment"* (John 16:8 KJV). The term here rendered *"reprove"* refers, in its proper sense, to judicial proceedings. When the judge has heard all the testimony and the arguments of counsel, he sums up the whole case and lays it before the jury, bringing out all the strong points, making all their condensed and accumulated power to influence the condemnation of the criminal. This is *reproving* him in the original and legitimate sense of the word used here by our Savior. In this way, the Holy Spirit *"reprove[s] the world of sin, and of righteousness, and of judgment."* In other words, the Spirit convinces or convicts the sinner by testimony, by argument, by arraying all the strong points of the case against him under solemn and powerful circumstances.

The Spirit-Filled Life

Proof of the Spirit's Striving

Our fourth question is, How may it be known when the Spirit of God strives with an individual? This is not known by direct perception of His agency through any of the physical senses, for His presence is not manifested to these organs. The Spirit's striving is also not known directly by our consciousness, for the only proper subjects of consciousness are the acts and states of our own minds. But we do know the presence and agency of the Spirit by His works. The results He produces are the legitimate proofs of His presence.

Attention Is Focused on the Soul

A person under the Spirit's influence finds his attention focused on the great concerns of his soul. Consider the case of a student who is studying his lesson. The solemn questions of duty and responsibility to God are continually intruding themselves upon his mind. His mind is continually drawn to think of God and of the judgment to come. He turns his attention back to his books, but soon it is off again. How can he neglect these matters so infinitely important to his future well-being?

So it is with all men and women; the Spirit of God turns the mind and draws it to God and the concerns of the soul. When such results take place, you may know that the Spirit of God is the cause. For who does not know that this drawing and inclining of the mind toward God is not natural to the human heart? When it does occur, therefore, we may know that the special agency of God is in it.

One Is Convinced of Sin in Himself

Again, when a man finds himself convinced of sin, he may know that this is the Spirit's work. Now, it is one thing to know oneself to be a sinner, but quite another to have the truth mightily take hold of the deepest places of the soul. When the latter takes place in a person, you may see his countenance fallen, his eyes downcast—his whole appearance is as if he had disgraced himself by some foul crime, or as if he had suddenly lost all the friends he ever had. I have often encountered impenitent sinners who looked condemned, as if conscious guilt had taken hold of their innermost soul. They were not aware that their faces revealed the deep workings of their hearts, but the observing eye could not help seeing it. I have also seen the same among backslidden believers, resulting from the same cause—the Spirit of God reproving them of sin.

Sometimes this conviction is of a general nature, and sometimes it is more specific. It may enforce only the general impression, "I am all wrong; I am utterly hateful to God; my whole heart is an abomination in His sight." In other cases, however, it may take hold of some particular form of sin, hold it up before the sinner's mind, and make him see his infinite repulsiveness before God for this sin. It may be a sin he has never thought of before, or he may have considered it as a very light matter; but now, through the Spirit, it rises up before his mind in such ugliness and loathsomeness that he abhors himself. He sees sin in a perfectly new light. He sees many things as sins now that he never deemed sins before.

The Mind Is Convicted of Sin's Guilt

Again, the Spirit not only convinces a person of the fact that certain things are sins, but He also convicts the mind of the great guilt and the ill consequences of sin. The sinner is made to feel that his sin deserves the most extreme damnation.

To illustrate this, let me present the case of an infidel I once knew. This man had lived in succession with two pious wives. He had read almost every book then in existence on the inspiration of the Scriptures. He had disputed against, objected to, and often thought himself to have triumphed over, believers in the Bible. In fact, he was the most subtle unbeliever I ever met. It was remarkable that, in connection with his unbelief, he had no proper views of sin. He had heard much about some dreadful depravity that had been passed down in human blood from Adam, and was itself a physical thing. But he had no oppressive consciousness of guilt for having his share of this original taint. Consequently, his mind was quite at ease regarding the guilt of his own sin.

But eventually a change came over him, and his eyes were opened to see the horrible enormity of his guilt. I saw him one day so borne down with sin and shame that he could not look up. He bowed his head upon his knees, covered his face, and groaned in agony. In this state I left him and went to a prayer meeting. Before long, he came into the meeting. As he left the meeting, he said to his wife, "You have long known me as a strong-hearted infidel; but my unbelief is all gone. I cannot tell you what has become of it—it all seems to me as absolute nonsense. I cannot imagine how I could ever have had such views and defended them. To myself, I seem like a man called to view some glorious and beautiful structure, in order to pass his judgment upon it, but who presumes to judge and condemn it after having caught only a dim glimpse of one obscure corner. I have done the same by condemning the glorious Bible and the glorious government of God."

All this change in his views about the Bible was the result of a change in his views about his own sin. Before, he had not been convicted of sin at all; now he saw it in some of its true light, and really felt that he deserved the deepest hell. Of course, he now saw the pertinence and beauty and glory of the gospel system. He was now in a position in which he could see clearly one of the strongest proofs of the truth of the Bible—namely, its perfect capacity to meet the needs of a sinning race.

Conviction of sin has a remarkable power to break up and annihilate the delusions of error. For instance, no man can thoroughly see his own sin and yet remain a Universalist, deeming it unjust for God to send him to hell. When I hear a man talking in defense of Universalism, I know that he does not understand anything about sin. He has not begun to see his own guilt in its true light. It is the blindest of all mental infatuations to think that the little inconveniences of this life are all that sin deserves. Let a man once see his own guilt, and he will be amazed to think that he ever held such a view. The Spirit of God, pouring light upon the sinner's mind, will soon render Universalism powerless.

I once labored in a village in the state of New York where Universalism prevailed extensively. The leading man among them had a sick wife who sympathized with his beliefs. She being near death, I went to see her and attempted to expose the utter fallacy of her delusion. After I had left, her husband returned. His wife, her eyes being now opened, cried out to him as he entered, "O my dear husband, you are on the way to hell! Your Universalism will ruin your soul forever!" He was greatly enraged, and when he learned that I had been talking with her, his rage was kindled against me. "Where is he now?" said he. "Gone to the meeting," was the reply. "I'll go there and shoot him," he cried; and seizing his loaded gun, as I was later informed, he started off. When he came in, I was preaching from the text, *"Serpents, brood of vipers! How can you escape the condemnation of hell?"* (Matt. 23:33). At the time, I knew nothing about his purpose—nothing about his gun. He listened awhile, and then all at once, in the midst of the meeting, he fell back on his seat and cried out, "Oh, I am sinking to hell! O God, have mercy on me." Away went his Universalism in an instant; he saw his sin and knew that he was sinking to hell. This change in him was not my work, for I could not produce effects such as these. I was indeed trying to show from my text what sinners deserve; but the Spirit of God, and nothing less, can bring about this sort of conviction of sin.

A Hard Heart Is Softened

Another fruit of the Spirit is developed in the case of those persons who are conscious of great hardness of heart. It often happens that men suppose themselves to be Christians because they have so much sensitivity toward religious subjects. To undeceive them, the Spirit directs their attention to some truth that dries up all their sensitivity and leaves their hopes stranded. Now they are in great agony. "The more I hear," they say, "the less I feel. I was never so far from being convicted of sin. I will certainly go to hell. I do not have a particle of feeling. I could not feel even if I were to die."

Now, the explanation of this state is usually this: the Spirit of God sees their danger—sees them deceiving themselves by relying on their feelings, and therefore brings some truths before their minds that set the opposition of their hearts against God and dry up the fountains of their sensitivity. Then they see how perfectly callous their hearts are toward God. This is the work of the Spirit.

The Soul Is Convicted of Unbelief

Again, the Spirit convicts the soul of the guilt of unbelief. Sinners are very likely to suppose that they believe the Gospel. They confuse faith with a merely intellectual assent to the facts. Thus blinded, they suppose that they believe God in the sense of gospel faith.

But the moment the Spirit reveals their own hearts to them, they will see that they do not believe in God as they believe in their fellowmen. Instead of having confidence in God and resting on His words of promise as they do on men's promises, they do not *rest* on God at all, but are full of anxiety that God will fail to fulfill His own words. They see that instead of being childlike and trustful, they are full of concern, trouble, and, in fact, unbelief. Also, they see that this is a horribly guilty state of heart. They see the guilt of not resting in His promises—the horrible guilt of not believing with the heart every word God ever uttered.

This change is the work of the Spirit. Our Savior mentioned it as one of the effects brought about by the Spirit, that He will *"convict the world of sin...because they do not believe in Me"* (John 16:8–9). In fact, we find that this is one of the characteristic works of the Spirit. I recently conversed with a man who has been for many years a professing Christian, but has been living in the seventh chapter of the book of Romans. He remarked to me, "I have been thinking of this truth, that God cares for me and loves me, and has through Jesus Christ offered me eternal life. Now I see that I deserve to be damned if I do not believe." Stretching out his pale hand, he said with great energy, "I *ought* to go to hell if I will not believe." All this is the work of the Spirit—this making a man see the guilt and deserved punishment of unbelief, this making a sinner see that everything else is only straw compared with the eternal rock of God's truth.

One Sees the Danger of Dying in Sin

Again, the Spirit makes men see the danger of dying in their sins. A young man once said to me, "I am afraid to go to sleep at night, lest I should awake in hell." Sinners often know what this feeling is. I recall being so much agonized by this thought that I almost imagined myself to be dying on the spot! Oh, I can never express the terror and the agony of my soul in that hour! Sinner, if you have these feelings, it is a solemn time for you.

One Fears Being Given Up by God

Moreover, the Spirit makes sinners feel the danger of being given up by God. It often happens that sinners, convicted by the Spirit, are made to feel that if they are not given up already, they are in the most imminent peril of it, and they must rush for the gate of life now or never. They see that they have so sinned and have done so much to provoke God to give them over to Satan, that their last hope of being accepted is quickly dying away. Sinners, have any of you ever felt this way? Have you ever trembled in your soul, lest you should be given over to a reprobate mind (see Romans 1:28) before another Sunday, or perhaps before another morning goes by? If so, you may ascribe this conviction to the Spirit of God.

One Is Convicted of Mental Blindness

Further, the Spirit often convicts sinners of the great blindness of their minds. It seems to them that their minds are full of solid darkness, as though it were a darkness that may be felt.

The Spirit Not Always Striving

This is really the natural state of the sinner, but he is not aware of it until he is enlightened by the Spirit of God. When thus enlightened, he begins to understand his own exceedingly great blindness. He now becomes aware that the Bible is a sealed book to him—for he finds that though he reads it, its meaning is enveloped in impenetrable darkness. (See Isaiah 29:11.)

Haven't some of you had an experience like this? Haven't you read the Bible with the distressing awareness that your mind was by no means suitably affected by its truth—indeed, with the conviction that you did not get hold of its truth to any good purpose at all? In this way, men and women are enlightened by the Spirit to see the real state of their case.

One Is Shown His Total Alienation from God

Again, the Spirit shows sinners their total alienation from God. I have seen sinners so strongly convicted of this, that they would say, "I know that I do not have the least inclination to return to God. I am conscious that I don't care whether I have any religion or not."

I have often seen professing Christians in this state, conscious that their hearts are utterly alienated from God and from all sympathy with His character or government. Their deep backslidings, or their utter lack of all religion, has been so revealed to their minds by the Spirit, as to become a matter of most distinct and impressive consciousness.

When the Spirit has made sinners to see themselves this way, they often find that when they pour out their words before God in prayer, their hearts "won't go." I once said to a sinner, "Come, now, give up your heart to God." "I will," he said, but in a moment he said, "My heart won't go." Haven't some of you been compelled to

91

say the same, "My heart won't go"? Then you know by experience one of the fruits of the Spirit's convicting power.

When the Spirit of God is not with men, they can dole out their long prayers before God and never think or seem to care how prayerless their hearts are all the time, and how utterly far from God. But when the Spirit sheds His light on the soul, the sinner sees how black a hypocrite he is. Oh, then he cannot pray so smoothly, so loosely, so self-complacently.

One Is Convinced of Being Ashamed of Christ

Again, the Spirit of God often convinces men that they are ashamed of Christ, and that in truth they do not wish for religion. It sometimes happens that sinners think there is no shame in seriously looking into the matter of salvation, until they actually come to be convicted. Such was the case with myself. I bought my first Bible as a law book, and studied it as I would any other law book, my sole purpose being to find in it the great principles of law. Then I never once thought of being ashamed of reading it. I read it as freely and as openly as I read any other book. But as soon as I became awakened to the concerns of my soul, I put my Bible out of sight. If it were lying on my table when people came into my office, I was careful to throw a newspaper over it. Before long, however, the conviction that I was ashamed of God and of His Word came over me with overwhelming force, and this served to show me the horrible state of my mind toward God. I suppose that the general course of my experience is by no means uncommon among impenitent sinners.

One Is Convicted of Worldly-mindedness

The Spirit also convicts men of worldly-mindedness. Sinners are always in this state of mind, but they are often not fully aware of the fact until the Spirit of God makes them see it. I have often seen men pursuing their worldly projects most intensely, but when asked about these projects they would say, "I don't care much about the world; I am pursuing this business just now chiefly because I want to be doing something." But when the Spirit shows them their own hearts, they are in agony, lest they will never be able to break away from the dreadful power of the world upon their souls. Now they see that they have been utter slaves on earth—slaves to the passion for worldly good.

The Truth Is Personally Applied

Again, the Holy Spirit often makes such a personal application of the truth that the sinner feels that the preacher, during a sermon, is describing his exact case and character. The individual thus convinced of sin may think that the preacher has, in some way, come to a knowledge of his character, and intends to describe it. The sinner believes that the preacher is talking about *him*, and is preaching to *him*. He wonders who has told the preacher so much about him. All this often takes place when the preacher perhaps does not know that such an individual is in the audience, and is altogether ignorant of his history. Thus, the Holy Spirit, who knows his heart and his entire history, becomes very personal in the application of truth.

Have any of you had this experience? Has it at any time appeared to you as if the preacher meant *you*, and that he was describing your case? Then the Spirit of the living God is upon you. I have often seen individuals, under my preaching, drop their heads almost as if they had been shot. In some cases, they were unable to look up again during the whole service. I have often heard afterward that they thought I meant them, and that others thought so, too. These individuals imagined that many eyes were turned on them, and therefore they did not look up, when in fact neither myself nor anyone in the congregation, in all probability, so much as thought of them.

In this way, a bow drawn at random often lodges an arrow between the joints of the sinner's armor. Sinner, is it so with you?

One Is Convinced of His Heart's Enmity against God

Again, the Holy Spirit often convinces sinners of the enmity of their hearts against God. Most impenitent sinners, and perhaps all professing Christians who are deceived, unless convinced to the contrary by the Holy Spirit, imagine that they are, on the whole, receptive toward God. They are far from believing that this *"carnal mind is enmity against God"* (Rom. 8:7). They think they do not hate God but, on the contrary, that they love God. Now, this delusion must be torn away or they must be lost. To do this, the Spirit so orders it that some truths are presented that show the sinner his real enmity against God.

Perhaps a man has a pious wife who has, like himself, thought him to be almost a Christian. Suppose the Holy Spirit begins to work in him. The man will begin by objecting to the truth, finding fault with the requirements and rules of it. Then he will refuse to go to church, and finally he will forbid his wife and family to go. Often his enmity of heart will boil over in a horrible manner. Perhaps he has no thought that this boiling up of hell within him is brought about by the Holy Spirit revealing to him the true state of his heart. His Christian friends may also mistake his case and believe him when he says that something is wrong in the subject matter or the manner of the preacher that is doing this man a great injury.

But beware what you say or do. In many such cases that I have observed, it has turned out that the Holy Spirit was at work in those hearts, revealing to them their real enmity against God. He does this by presenting truth in such a manner and under such circumstances that these results will be produced. He pushes this process until He compels the soul to see that it is filled with enmity toward God and toward what is right. He causes the sinner to see that it is not man, but God, to whom he is opposed; that it is not error, but truth; not the manner, but the matter; not the requirements, but the God of truth whom he hates.

One Is Convicted of His Heart's Deceitfulness

The Spirit, moreover, often convicts sinners powerfully of the deceitfulness of their own hearts. Sometimes this conviction becomes truly appalling. Sinners see that they have been deluding themselves in matters too plain to justify any mistake, and too important to allow for any defense of their willful blindness. They are baffled by what they see in themselves.

One Is Stripped of His Excuses

The Spirit also often strips the sinner of his excuses, and shows him clearly their great foolishness and absurdity. This was one of the first things in my experience in the process of conviction. I lost all confidence in any of my excuses, for I found them to be so foolish and futile that I could not endure them. This was my state of mind before I had ever heard of the Spirit's work, or knew at all how to determine whether my own mind was under

His influence or not. I found that although I had been very strong in my excuses and objections, I was now utterly weak, and it seemed to me that any child could overthrow me. In fact, I did not need to be overthrown by anybody, for my excuses and objections had sunk to nothing by themselves, and I was deeply ashamed of them. I had essentially worked myself out of all their mazes, so that they could bewilder me no longer. Since that time, I have seen multitudes in the same condition—their excuses weakened, their old defensive armor all torn off, and their hearts laid naked to the arrows of God's truth.

Now, sinners, have any of you known what this is— to have all your excuses and defenses failing you, to feel that you have no courage and no legitimate reasons for pushing forward in a course of sin? If so, then you know what it is to be under the convicting power of the Spirit.

One Is Convicted That Christ Is the Only Savior

The Spirit convicts men of the foolishness of seeking salvation in any other way than through Christ alone. Often, without being aware of it, a sinner will be really seeking salvation in some other way than through Christ; he will be looking to his good deeds, or to his own prayers, or to the prayers of some Christian friends. But if the Spirit ever brings this sinner to true salvation, He will tear away these delusive schemes and show him the utter vanity of every other way than through Christ alone. The Spirit will show him that there is only this one way in which it is possible for a sinner to be saved, and that all attempts at salvation by any other way are forever in vain and worse than worthless. All self-righteousness must be rejected entirely, and Christ be sought alone.

Have you ever been made to see this? You who are professing Christians, is this your experience?

One Knows the Foolishness of an Unsanctifying Hope

Again, the Spirit convinces men of the great foolishness and madness of clinging to an unsanctifying hope. The Bible teaches that everyone who has the genuine gospel hope purifies himself, even as Christ is pure (1 John 3:3). Let's look at the passage in which the apostle John wrote about this hope:

> *Beloved, now we are children of God; and it has not yet been revealed what we shall be, but we know that when He is revealed, we shall be like Him, for we shall see Him as He is. And everyone who has this hope in Him purifies himself, just as He is pure.* (1 John 3:2–3)

In this passage, John plainly meant to affirm a universal characteristic of the Christian hope. Whoever has a Christian hope should ask, "Do I purify myself even as Christ is pure?" If not, then he does not have the true gospel hope.

Thousands of professing Christians have a most inefficient hope. What is this hope? Does it really lead them to purify themselves as Christ is pure? Nothing of the sort. It is not a hope that they will see Christ *"as He is,"* and be forever with Him, and be altogether *"like Him,"* too. Rather, it is mainly a hope that they will escape hell and will go to some unknown heaven as an alternative.

Such so-called Christians must know that they lack the witness of their own consciences that they are living for God and bearing His image. If such people are ever to be saved, they must first be convinced of the foolishness of a hope that leaves them unsanctified.

The Spirit-Filled Life

You who claim to be Christians but who have lived a worldly life so long, are you not ashamed of your hope? Do you not have good reason to be ashamed of a hope that has no more power than yours has had? Are there not many of you who, in the honesty of your hearts, must say, "Either there is no power in the Gospel, or I don't know anything about it"? For regarding all those who are not under the law, but under grace, the Gospel affirms as a universal fact that *"sin shall not have dominion over you"* (Rom. 6:14). Now, will you go before God and say, "Lord, You have said, *'Sin shall not have dominion over you,'* but, Lord, that is all false. I believe the Gospel and am under grace, but sin still has dominion over me"? No doubt there is a mistake somewhere in this case, and it would be wise to ask yourself solemnly, "Will I blame this mistake and falsehood upon God, or will I admit that it must be in myself alone?"

The apostle Paul said, *"The gospel...is the power of God to salvation for everyone who believes"* (Rom. 1:16). Is it so to you?

Paul also said, *"Having been justified by faith, we have peace with God through our Lord Jesus Christ"* (Rom. 5:1). Do you know this in your own experience? Paul added that we

> rejoice in hope of the glory of God. And not only that, but we also glory in tribulations, knowing that tribulation produces perseverance; and perseverance, character; and character, hope. Now hope does not disappoint, because the love of God has been poured out in our hearts by the Holy Spirit who was given to us. (Rom. 5:2–5)

Dear Christian, is all this in accordance with your experience? Is it true that your hope *"does not disappoint"*?

Does it produce the glorious fruits unto holiness that are described here? If you were to try your experience by the Word of the living God, and open your heart to be searched by the Spirit, would you not be convinced that you do not truly embrace the Gospel?

One Is Convinced That He Is Entirely Selfish

Again, the Spirit convinces men that all their goodness is selfish, and that self is the end of all their efforts, their prayers, and their religious practices. I once spent a little time with a man who was a leading member in a Presbyterian church. He said to me, "What would you think of a man who is praying for the Spirit every day, but does not get the blessing?" I answered, "I would presume that he is praying selfishly." "But suppose," he replied, "that he is praying for the sake of promoting his own happiness?" "He may be purely selfish in that," I replied, adding, "The Devil might do as much, and perhaps he would do just the same if he supposed he could make himself happier by it." I then cited the prayer of David: *"Do not take Your Holy Spirit from me. Restore to me the joy of Your salvation....Then I will teach transgressors Your ways, and sinners shall be converted to You"* (Ps. 51:11–13). This seemed to be new doctrine to him.

I found out afterward that he turned away from our discussion in great anger and trouble. In the first gush of feeling, he prayed that God would cut him down and send him to hell, lest he should have to confess his sin and shame before all the people. He saw that, in fact, his past religion had been all selfish; but the dread of confessing this was at first appalling. He saw, however, the possibility of being mistaken, that his hopes had been all delusive, and that he had been working his self-deceived course fast down toward the depths of hell.

One Feels That This Is His Last Chance

Finally, it is the Spirit's work to make self-deceived individuals feel that they are now hearing their last call from the Spirit. When this impression is made, it should by all means be heeded. It is God's own voice to the soul. Out of the many cases I have observed in which God has distinctly made sinners feel that the present call was their last, I do not recall one in which it did not prove to be so. This is a solemn truth to the sinner, and it ought to make the warning voice of God ring in his ear like the forewarning knell of the second death.

He Will Not Strive Forever

Our fifth question is, What is intended by the Spirit's "not always striving"? I take the meaning of this to be, not that He will at some period withdraw from among mankind, but that He will withdraw from the individual in question, or perhaps from a whole generation of sinners. In its general application now, the principle seems to be that the Spirit will not follow the sinner down to his grave, that there will be a limit to His efforts in the case of each sinner, and that this limit is reached a longer or a shorter time before death. At some uncertain, awful point, he will reach and pass it; therefore, it would be wise for every sinner to understand his peril of grieving the Spirit forever away.

Why the Spirit Will Not Always Strive

Our next inquiry is, Why will God's Spirit not always strive with man? I answer, not because God is not compassionate, patient, slow to anger, and great in mercy (Ps. 103:8); not because He becomes impatient and acts unreasonably—no, nothing of this sort at all. Let me tell you the reasons why God's Spirit will not always strive with sinners.

It Will Do the Sinner No Good

First, the Spirit will not always strive because striving longer will do the sinner no good. Conversion must be brought about through the influence of truth. But when truth is resisted time and again, it loses its power upon the mind that resists it. Every successive instance of resistance weakens its power. If the truth does not take hold with energy when it is fresh, it is not likely ever to do so. Thus, when the Spirit reveals truth to the sinner, and he hardens himself against it and resists the Spirit, there remains little hope for him. We may expect God to give him up for lost. This is what the Bible teaches.

It Worsens the Sinner's Case

If we ask again, Why does God cease to strive with sinners? the answer may be, Because to strive longer not only does the sinner no good, but it makes the case far worse. Guilt increases as light increases; the more light, the greater guilt. Thus, more light revealed by the Spirit and longer striving might serve only to increase the sinner's guilt, and of course his final misery. After all hope of his repentance is gone, it is better for the sinner that the Spirit should leave him, than that His efforts should be prolonged in vain, only to increase the sinner's light and guilt, and consequently his endless curse. In this case, it is a real mercy to the sinner when God withdraws His Spirit and lets him alone.

Sinners Willfully Sin by Resisting the Spirit

Third, the Spirit will not always strive because sinners sin willfully when they resist the Holy Spirit. It is the work of the Spirit to throw light before their minds; therefore, in resisting the Spirit, they must sin against light—hence their dreadful guilt.

We are often greatly shocked by the bold and daring sins of men who, after all, have little illumination of the Spirit and of course comparatively little guilt. But when God's ministers come to the souls of men with His messages of truth, and men despise or neglect them; when God's providence also enforces His truth, and still men resist, they are greatly guilty. How much more so when God comes by His Spirit, and they resist God under the blazing light of His Spirit's illuminations! How infinitely increased is their guilt now!

Resistance Tempts God's Patience

Fourth, their resistance tempts the patience of God. Never do sinners so grievously tempt the patience of God as when they resist His Spirit. You may see this illustrated in the response of the Jews of Stephen's time. Stephen said to them, *"You stiffnecked and uncircumcised in heart and ears! You always resist the Holy Spirit; as your fathers did, so do you"* (Acts 7:51). In his speech to them, he had gone down the track of their national history, running fearlessly across their Jewish prejudices and laboring in the deep sincerity and faithfulness of his soul to set before them their guilt in persecuting and murdering the Son of God. And what did they do? Enraged at these rebukes, they gnashed at him with their teeth, set upon him with the spirit of demons, and stoned him to death, although they saw the glory of God beaming in his eyes and on his face as if it had been an angel's. (See Acts 7:54–60.)

Did not this fearful deed of theirs seal up the destruction of the Jewish nation? Read the history of their nation and see. They had tempted God to the last limit of His patience; now what remained for them but swift and awful judgment? The wrath of God arose against them, and there was no remedy. Their resistance of the Holy Spirit tested the patience of God until it could bear no more.

It is a solemn truth that sinners tempt God's patience most dangerously when they resist His Spirit. Think how long some of you have resisted the Holy Spirit. The claims of God have been presented to you again and again, but you have as often put them away. You have said to God, *"Depart from us, for we do not desire the knowledge of Your ways"* (Job 21:14). Now, do you not have the utmost reason to expect that God will take you at your word?

Patience Cannot Be Unlimited

Fifth, God's Spirit will stop striving because there is a point beyond which patience is no virtue. This is true in all governments. No government could possibly be maintained that remained patient toward the guilty beyond all limits. There must be a point beyond which God cannot go without peril to His government; we may be assured that He will never pass over this point.

Suppose that old, gray-headed sinners were converted as often as youthful sinners are, and that this were the general course of things. Would this not bring ruin to God's government—ruin even to sinners themselves? Would not sinners take encouragement from this and continue in their sins until their lusts were worn out, and until they themselves were rotted down in their corruptions? They would say, "We will be just as likely to be converted in our old age, putrid with long-indulged lusts, and rank from the unchecked growth of every abomination of the heart of man, as if we were to turn to

God in the freshness of our youth. Therefore, let us have the pleasures of sin first, and the unwelcomeness of religion when the world can give us no more to enjoy."

But God generally intends to have men and women converted young if at all. One reason for this is that He intends to convert the world, and therefore must have laborers trained up for the work in the morning of life. If He were to make no distinction between the young and the old, converting from each class alike, or chiefly from the elderly, the means for converting the world would utterly fail. Therefore, there is a necessity for the general fact that sinners must submit to God in early life.

The Consequences of the Spirit's Not Striving

Now, what are the consequences of the Spirit's ceasing to strive with men?

Hardness of Heart

One consequence will be a confirmed hardness of heart. It is inevitable that the heart will become much more hardened, and the will more fully set to do evil.

Opposition to Religion

Another consequence will be a confirmed opposition to religion. This will be likely to manifest itself in people's dislike of everything on the subject, often with great impatience and irritability when pressed to pay attention to the subject seriously. Perhaps they will refuse to have anything said to themselves personally, so settled is their opposition to God and His claims.

Opposition to Revivals and Ministers

You may also expect to see them opposed to revivals and to gospel ministers, and preeminently to those ministers who are most faithful to their souls. All the means of promoting revivals and rousing the conscience will be peculiarly hateful to their hearts. Usually such individuals become sour in their dispositions, cynical, haters of all Christians, delighting in slandering and abusing those whose piety annoys and disturbs their stupid complacency in sin.

Escape to a Refuge of Lies

Another consequence of being forsaken by the Spirit is that men will escape to some refuge of lies, and will settle down in some form of fatal error. I have often thought it almost impossible for men to heartily embrace fatal error unless they are first forsaken by the Spirit of God.

After having observed a number of cases, I believe this to be the case with the great majority of Universalists. They are described by Paul: *"They* [do] *not receive the love of the truth, that they might be saved. And for this reason God will send them strong delusion, that they should believe the lie"* (2 Thess. 2:10–11). They hate the truth; they are more than willing to be deceived; they are fidgety when pressed with gospel claims; therefore, they are ready to grasp at any form of delusion that sets aside these claims and boldly asserts, *"You will not surely die"* (Gen. 3:4). It has long been an impression in my mind that this is the usual course of feeling and thought that leads to Universalism. There may be exceptions, but the majority of its followers go into this delusion from the starting point of being abandoned by the Spirit. Thus abandoned, they become cross and cynical—they hate all Christians and all the truths that God and His people love. This could not be the case if they had the love of God in their hearts. It could not well be the case if they were enlightened and controlled by the present agency of the Divine Spirit.

A Seared Conscience

Again, generally those who are left by God come to have a seared conscience. They are distinguished by great insensitivity of the mind. By their own choice, they are blind and hardened in respect to the nature and guilt of sin. Although their intelligence affirms that sin is wrong, they do not feel it or care about it. They can know the truth and yet be reckless of its application to their own hearts and lives. God has left them, and of course then the natural tendencies of a depraved heart are developed without restraint.

Becoming Worse All the Time

Again, this class of sinners will inevitably grow worse and worse. They become loose in habits and lax in their observance of the Sabbath. They slide backwards in regard to abstinence from alcohol, and all similar moral subjects. They slip into some of the many forms of sin and perhaps vice and crime. If they have been conscientious against the use of tobacco, they relinquish their conscientiousness and throw a loose rein on their lusts. In short, they are likely to become worse and worse in every branch of morals, and often become so changed that you would hardly recognize them. It will be no strange thing if they become profane swearers, or if they steal a little now and a good deal later. And if God does not restrain them, they go down by a short and steep descent to the depths of hell.

Certain Damnation

Another consequence of being abandoned by the Spirit will be certain damnation. There can be no mistake about this. It is just as certain as if the sinner were already in hell.

This state of knowing one will be damned is not always accompanied by apathy. At times, there may be a most intense excitement of the emotions. The Bible describes the case of some who *"sin willfully after* [they] *have received the knowledge of the truth,* [for whom] *there no longer remains a sacrifice for sins, but a certain fearful expectation of judgment, and fiery indignation"* (Heb. 10:26–27). I have seen some individuals who fit this description, and such agony and such wretchedness I pray I may never see again. I have seen them, the very pictures of despair and horror, their eyes open fully to see their ruined state, exclaiming, "I know I am abandoned by God forever. I have sinned away my day of hope and mercy, and I know I never will repent. I have no heart to repent, although I know that I must, or be damned." They utter these words with a settled tone, and with an air of agony and despair that is enough to break a heart of stone.

Prayers Cannot Be Offered for Them

Another consequence often is that Christians find themselves unable to pray in faith for such sinners. There are some people in almost every community for whom Christians cannot pray. I believe it is common for many Christians, without being aware of each other's state, to have a similar experience at one time. For example, several Christians are each praying in secret for a certain individual, and then they suddenly find that they can no longer pray for him. They happen to meet, and one says, "I have been praying a long time with great interest for this certain impenitent sinner, but at a particular time I found myself all shut up; I could not get hold of the Lord again for him, and never have been able to since." Another says, "I have felt the same way. I did not know that anyone else felt as I have, but you have described my case precisely."

Now, if you will go to that sinner, he will tell you a story that will explain the whole case and show that, at that eventful moment, he came to some fatal decision, grieved the Spirit, and was abandoned by God. The Spirit ceased to strive with him, and consequently ceased to draw forth prayer on his behalf in the hearts of God's people.

Point of No Return

Finally, when God has ceased to strive with sinners, no means whatsoever can be effective in leading them to salvation. If you, sinner, have passed that dreadful point, you will gain nothing by my preaching even if I were to preach five thousand sermons to you. Indeed, you could not benefit from an angel, or even Christ Himself, coming and preaching to you. All would be only in vain. You are left by God to fill up the measure of your iniquities.

REMARKS

1. From what I have said, Christians may understand how to account for the fact that there are some sinners for whom they cannot pray. Even while they are walking with God, and trying to pray for particular individuals, they may find themselves utterly unable to do so; and this may be the explanation. In such a case, however, I would not take it for granted that all is right with myself, for perhaps it is not. But if I do have the

best evidence that all is right between myself and God, then I must infer that God has forsaken that sinner and does not wish me to pray any longer for him.

2. Sinners should be aware that light and guilt keep pace with each other. They are increased and lessened together. Hence, there is a solemn responsibility of being under the light and the strivings of the Spirit.

While enlightened and pressed to duty by the Spirit, sinners are under the most solemn circumstances that can ever occur in their lives. Indeed, no period of the sinner's existence through its eternal duration can be so momentous as this. Yes, sinner, while the Spirit of God is pleading and striving with you, angels appreciate the solemnity of the hour—they know that the destiny of your soul is being decided for eternity. What an object of infinite interest! An immortal mind on the pivot of its eternal destiny—God debating and persuading, the sinner resisting, and the struggle about to be broken off as hopeless forever.

Sinner, suppose you could set yourself aside and be a spectator of such a scene. Were you ever in a court of justice when the question of life and death was about to be decided? The witnesses have all been heard; the counsel have been heard; it is announced that the members of the jury are ready to deliver their verdict. Now pause and take in the scene. Note the anxiety depicted in every face, and how eagerly and yet with what awful solemnity they wait for the decision about to be made. And there is good reason for this, for a question of great interest is to be decided. But if this question, involving only the temporal life, is so momentous, how much more so is the sinner's case, when the life of the soul for eternity is pending! Oh, how solemn while the question still pends—while the Spirit still strives, the sinner resists, and no one can tell how soon the last moment of the Spirit's striving may come!

This earth ought to be the most solemn world in the universe. In other worlds, the destinies of the souls are already settled. It is so in hell; everything there is settled and changeless forever. It is a solemn thing indeed for a sinner to go to hell, but the most solemn point in the whole duration of his existence is the one in which the decision is made.

Oh, what a world this is! Throughout all its years and centuries, there is not one moment on which there does not hang the question of eternal life or eternal death! Is this a place to be mad and foolish and vain? No! It would be more reasonable to treat everything as trivial in any other world than in this one. The solemn destinies of the soul are being determined here. Heaven and hell see it, and all are filled with concern, swelling almost to agony. But you who are the subjects of all this anxiety— you continue to treat this matter lightly and play the fool and dance on the brink of everlasting woe.

God represents the sinner as on a slippery slope, his feet just sliding on the edge of an awful chasm (Ps. 73:18–20). God holds him up for a short time, but the sinner squanders even this short moment in mad foolishness. All hearts in heaven and in hell are beating and throbbing with intense emotion, but he is reckless! Oh, what madness!

If sinners properly estimated this danger of resisting the Spirit, they would be more afraid of it than of anything else whatsoever. They would consider no other danger worthy of a moment's thought or care compared with this.

3. It is a very common thing for sinners to grieve away the Spirit long before death. I believe this, although

some people are greatly opposed to this doctrine. Do you doubt it? Think of almost the whole Jewish nation in the time of the Savior. They were given up to unbelief and abandoned by the Spirit of God, yet they sinned against far less light and of course with much less guilt than sinners do now. If God could give them up then, why may He not do so with sinners now? If He could give up the whole population of the world in Noah's time, when Noah was the only preacher of righteousness, why may He not now give up individual sinners who are incomparably more guilty than they, because they have sinned against greater light than had ever shone then?

Oh, it is infinitely cruel to sinners to hide this truth from them! Let them know that they are in danger of grieving away the Spirit forever, long before they die. This truth ought to be proclaimed over all the earth. Let it ring out through every valley and over every mountaintop, the world around. Let every living sinner hear it and take the timely warning!

4. We see why so few elderly sinners are converted. The fact is striking and unquestionable. Count the number of people converted past the age of sixty. You will find it small indeed. They are few and scattered, like beacons on mountaintops, just barely enough to prevent the aged from utter despair of ever being converted. I am aware that unbelievers use this fact to rail against religion, saying, "Why do the aged and wise, whose minds are developed by thought and experience, and who have passed the period of youthful passion, never embrace the Gospel?" They would gladly say that no one but children and women become religious, and that this is because the Christian religion rests on its appeal to the emotions, and not to the intelligence.

But unbelievers make a flagrant mistake in this inference. There is an entirely different class of causes for this fact. The aged are rarely converted, because they have grieved away the Spirit—they have become entangled in the mazes of some loved and soul-ruinous delusion; they are hardened in sin, past the moral possibility of being converted. Indeed, it would be unwise on God's part to convert many sinners in old age; then, at all the earlier periods of life, sinners would be looking forward to old age as the time for conversion. It would be too great a temptation for human nature to bear.

I have already said what I wish to repeat here—that it is a truly momentous time when God's Spirit strives with sinners. Perhaps the Spirit is striving with some of you. Even within the past week, God has been calling upon you to repent and has gotten your attention. Are you aware that while God is calling, you must listen— that when He speaks, you should pause and give Him your attention? Dear student, God is calling you away from your lesson, and are you replying, "Oh, I must, I *must* get back to my lesson"? Ah, your lesson! What is to be your first and chief lesson? *"Prepare to meet your God"* (Amos 4:12). But you insist, "The bell will toll in a few minutes, and I have not finished my lesson!" Yes, sinner, soon the great bell *will* toll—unseen spirits will take hold of the rope and toll the dreaded death-knell of eternity, echoing the summons, "Come to judgment." And when the bell tolls for you, sinner—as indeed it will—where will you be? Are you prepared? Have you gotten that one great lesson, *"Prepare to meet your God"*?

In the long-elapsing ages of your doom, you will be asked how and why you came into this place of torment. You will have to answer, "Oh, I was studying my lesson when God came by His Spirit, and I could not stop to hear His call! So I exchanged my soul for my lesson! Oh, what a fool I was!"

The Spirit Not Always Striving

Let me ask the people of God, Should you not be awake in such an hour as this? How many sinners during the past week have asked you to pray for their perishing souls? Have you no heart to pray? How full of danger are these critical moments!

Sinners, think of your destiny, now about to assume its fixed position. Soon you will decide it forever and forever!

Do you say, "First let me think about it, and then I will give myself up to God"? No, sinner, *no!* Do not go on in your sin, for *"now is the accepted time"* (2 Cor. 6:2)— now, today—*now* is the only hour of promise—now is perhaps the last hour of the Spirit's presence and grace to your soul!

Chapter 6

God's Love Commended to Us

But God commendeth his love toward us,
in that, while we were yet sinners, Christ died for us.
—Romans 5:8 KJV

What is meant here by *"commendeth"*? The word *commend* means "to recommend; to set forth in a clear and strong light." Toward whom is this love exercised? Toward us—toward all beings of our lost human race. He manifests this love to each one of us. Is it not written, *"God so loved the world that He gave His only begotten Son, that whoever believes in Him should not perish but have everlasting life"* (John 3:16)?

How God Demonstrates His Love

How does God commend this love? By having given His Son to die for us, by having given One who was a well-beloved Son. It is written that God *"gave [Him as] a ransom for all"* (1 Tim. 2:6) and that He tasted death for everyone (Heb. 2:9). We are not to suppose that He died for all of mankind in such a sense that His death is not truly for each one in particular. This is a great mistake into which some fall, to suppose that Christ died for the human race in general, but not for each one in particular. By this mistake, the Gospel is likely to lose much of its practical power on our hearts. We need to understand it as Paul did, who said of Jesus Christ, *"The Son of God...loved me and gave Himself for me"* (Gal. 2:20). We need to make this personal application of Christ's death. No doubt this was the great secret of Paul's holy life, and of his great power in preaching the Gospel. In the same way, we are to regard Jesus as having loved us personally and individually. Consider the effort God has put forth to make us feel that He cares for us personally. It is so in His providence, and also in His Gospel. He would happily make us separate ourselves from the majority and feel that His loving eyes and heart are upon us individually.

Why God Demonstrates His Love

For what purpose does God commend His love to us? Is it an ambition to make a display? No, surely there can be no artificiality in this. God is infinitely above all artificiality. From His very nature, He must act honestly. Thus, God must have some good reason for this manifestation of His love.

To Prove Its Reality

No doubt He seeks to prove to us the reality of His love. Feeling the most perfect love toward our lost race, He deemed it best to reveal this love both to us and to all His creatures. And what could reveal His love, if this gift of His Son does not? Oh, how gloriously is love revealed in this great sacrifice! How this makes divine love stand out prominently before the universe! What else could He have done that would prove His love so effectively?

God's Love Commended to Us

To Prove Its Unselfishness

Also, God wishes to show that His love is unselfish, for Jesus did not die for us as friends, but as enemies. It was while we were yet enemies that He died for us (Rom. 5:10). On this point, Paul suggested that *"scarcely for a righteous man will one die; yet perhaps for a good man someone would even dare to die"* (v. 7). But human beings were as far as possible from being good. Indeed, they were not even righteous, but were utterly wicked. For a very dear friend, one might be willing to die. There have been soldiers who, to save the life of a beloved officer, have taken into their own hearts the shaft of death. But for one who is not even good, this sacrifice could scarcely be made. How much less for an enemy! In this we may see how greatly *"God commendeth his love toward us, in that, while we were yet sinners, Christ died for us."*

Furthermore, God's love for us is not based on His being satisfied with us or having a high opinion of us. There is no basis in us for such a love. Thus, God's love can be nothing but the love of unselfish benevolence. This love has been called into question before. Satan questioned it in Eden. He boldly insinuated, *"'Has God indeed said, "You shall not eat of every tree of the garden"?'* (Gen. 3:1). Why would God wish to hold you back from such a pleasure?" In this way, the old Serpent attempted to cast suspicion on the benevolence of God. This gave God all the more reason to vindicate His love.

To Prove Its Strength

God also wished to commend the great strength of this love. We often think that to give a friend a great sum of money is to show evidence of strong love. But what is any sum of money compared with giving up a dear Son to die? Oh, surely it is surpassing love, wonderful beyond measure, that Jesus not only labored and suffered, but also really *died!* Was ever love like this?

To Reveal Its Moral Character

Again, God also intended to reveal the moral character of His love for mankind, and especially its justice. He could not show leniency to the guilty until His government was made secure and His law was properly honored. Without this sacrifice, He knew it could not be safe to pardon. God must maintain the honor of His throne. He must show that He could never ignore sin. He felt the solemn necessity of giving a public rebuke of sin before the universe. This rebuke was all the more expressive because Jesus Himself was sinless. Of course, in Christ's death, God was not frowning on His sin, but on the sin of those whose sins He bore and in whose place He stood.

Jesus stood as our Representative. While Christ stood in this position, God could not spare Him, but laid on Him the chastisement of our iniquities. (See Isaiah 53:5.) Oh, what a rebuke of sin that was! How expressively it showed that God abhorred sin, yet loved the sinner! These were among the great purposes He had in mind—to create in our souls the twofold conviction of *His* love for us and of *our* sin against Him. He wanted to make those convictions strong and abiding. So He set forth Jesus crucified before our eyes—a far more expressive thing than any mere words. Simply saying that He loved us could not approximate the strength and impressiveness of this manifestation. In no other way could He make it seem so much a reality—so touching and so overpowering.

In this way, God commends His love to us and invites us to look at it. He tells us that angels desire to look into it (1 Pet. 1:12). He wants us to weigh this great fact, examine all its implications, until it falls full upon our souls with its power to save. He commends it so that it will be reciprocated, so that we will be stirred up to love Him who has so loved us. He wants us to understand this love, to appreciate it, so that we may love Him in return. It is an example for us so that we may love our enemies and, much more, our friends. Oh, when this love has taken its effect in our hearts, how deeply we feel that we cannot hate anyone for whom Christ died! Then we love our neighbor with a love so deep and so pure that it cannot be in our heart to do him wrong.

To Show What True Love Is

It was thus a part of the divine purpose to show us what true love is. I once heard it said in prayer, "We thank You, Father, that You have given us Your Son to teach us how to love." Yes, God wants to let us know that He Himself is love (1 John 4:8); therefore, if we wish to be His children, we, too, must love Him and love one another. He desires to reveal His love so as to draw us into harmony with Himself and to make us more like Him. Do you not suppose that a thorough consideration of God's love, as manifested in Christ, teaches us what love is, and serves to draw our souls into such love? The question is often asked, How will I love? The answer is given in this example. Here is love! Look at it and drink in its spirit. Man is prone to love himself supremely. But here is a totally different sort of love. This love commends itself in that *while we were yet sinners, Christ died for us.* How forcibly this rebukes our selfishness! How much we need this lesson, to subdue our narrow selfishness and to shame our unbelief!

How strange it is that men do not realize the love of God! The wife of a minister, who had herself labored in many revivals, once said to me, "Until a few days ago, I never knew that God is love." "What do you mean?" I asked. "I mean that I never understood it in all its implications before." Oh, I assure you, it is a great and blessed truth, and it is a great thing to see it as it is! When it becomes a reality to the soul, and you come under its power, then you will find the Gospel is indeed *"the power of God to salvation"* (Rom. 1:16). Paul prayed for his Ephesian converts, that they might

> be able to comprehend with all the saints what is the width and length and depth and height; to know the love of Christ which passes knowledge; that [they might] be filled with all the fullness of God. (Eph. 3:18–19)

To Lessen Our Slavelike Fear of God

In thus commending His love to us, God sought to subdue our slavelike fear of Himself. Someone once said, "When I was young, I was aware of fearing God, but I knew I did not love Him. The instruction I received led me to fear, but not to love." As long as we think of God only as One to be feared, not to be loved, there will be a prejudice against Him as more an enemy than a friend. Every sinner knows that he deserves to be hated by God. He sees plainly that God must have good reason to be displeased with him. Knowing how he would feel toward one who had wronged him, he unconsciously infers that God must feel this way toward every sinner. When he tries to pray, his heart won't; he experiences nothing but terror. He feels no attraction toward God, no real love. The spirit of a child, on the other hand, comes before God weeping indeed, but loving and trusting.

God wishes to remove our deception and make us realize that, although He has spoken against us, He still

earnestly remembers us. (See Jeremiah 31:20.) God
wants us to interpret His dealings fairly and without
prejudice. He sees how, when He thwarts men's plans,
they are inclined toward misunderstanding Him. They
think that He does not care about their welfare, and they
are blind to the precious truth that He shapes all His
dealings with them in love and kindness. God wants us to
conclude that, if He did not spare His own Son, but gave
Him up freely for us all, then He will much more give us
all other things most freely (Rom. 8:32).

To Lead Us Out of Bondage into Love

Last, God wishes to lead us to serve Him in love and
not in bondage. He wants to draw us forth into the liberty of the sons of God (v. 21). He loves to see the obedience of the heart. He wants to inspire love enough to
make all our service cheerful and full of joy. If you wish
to make others love you, you must give them your love. If
you show your employees the love of your heart, their
service will be one of love. In this way, God commends
His love toward us in order to win our hearts to Himself,
and to prepare us to dwell forever in His eternal home.
His ultimate aim is to save us from our sins, so that He
may fill us forever with His own joy and peace.

REMARKS

1. We see that saving faith must be the heart's belief
of this great fact that God so loved us. Saving faith receives the death of Christ as an expression of God's love
to us. No other sort of faith—no faith in anything else—
wins our heart to love God. Saving faith saves us from

our bondage and our prejudice against Him. This is what makes it *saving*. Any faith that leaves out this great truth must fail to save us. If any one element of faith is vital, it is this. Let any man doubt this fact of God's love in Christ, and I would not give anything for all his religion. It is worthless.

2. The Old Testament system is full of this idea. All those bloody sacrifices are full of it. The priest, on behalf of all the people, came forward, laid his hand on the head of the innocent animal, then confessed his sins and the sins of all. When the animal was slain and its blood poured out before the Lord, and God gave a sign that He accepted the offering, it was a solemn manifestation that with the death of an innocent lamb, God substituted for the sufferings due the sinner. We find the same idea throughout that ancient system, showing how God desired that men would see His love in the gift of His own dear Son.

3. One great reason why men find it so difficult to repent and submit to God is that they do not receive this great fact—they do not accept it in simple faith. If they were to accept it and let it come home to their hearts, it would subdue their hearts to submission and to love.

4. One reason why young men are so afraid of being called into the ministry is their lack of confidence in this love. But if they saw and believed this great love, surely they would not let millions and millions go down to hell in ignorance of this Gospel! Oh, how it would agonize their hearts that so many would go to their graves and to an eternal hell, and never know the love of Jesus for their perishing souls! Yet here is a young man for whom Christ has died, who cannot bear to go and tell them they have a Savior! How much is his heart like Christ's heart?

Does it seem strange that Paul could not remain quiet, but felt that he must go to the ends of the earth and preach the name of Jesus where it had never been known before? How deeply he felt that he must let the world know these *"good tidings of great joy"* (Luke 2:10)! How startling that young men and women these days can let the Gospel die unknown and not go forth to bless the lost! Ah, did they ever taste its blessedness? Have they ever known its power? And do you solemnly intend to conceal it, that it may never bless your dying fellow-man?

5. This manner of commending God's love is the strongest and most expressive He could employ. In no other possible way could He so forcibly demonstrate His great love to the human race.

Hence, if this fails to subdue men's enmity, prejudice, and unbelief, what can? What methods will God use after this does not work? The Bible demands, *"How shall we escape if we neglect so great a salvation?"* (Heb. 2:3). The Bible has every right to make this appeal, for if this fails to win us, what can succeed?

6. If we had been His friends, there would have been no need of His dying for us. It was only because we were yet sinners that He died for us. How great, then, are the claims of this love on our hearts!

7. Sinners often think that if they were pious and good, the Lord might love them. So they try to win His love by doing some good things. They try in every way to make God love them, especially by mending their manners rather than their hearts. Unfortunately, they seem not to know that the very fact of their being sunk so low in sin is moving God's heart to its very foundations! A sinless angel enjoys God's satisfaction, but not His pity; he is not an object of pity, and there is no call for it. The same is true of a good child. He receives the satisfaction of his parents, but not their pity.

But suppose this child becomes vicious. Then his parents mourn over his fall, and their compassion is moved. They look on him with pity and anxiety as they see him going down to the depths of vice, crime, and degradation. More and more as he sinks lower and lower in the filth and abominations of sin, they mourn over him; and as they see how changed he is, they are full of tears, saying, "This is our son, our once-honored son! But how fallen he is now! Our hearts are moved for him, and there is nothing we would not do or suffer, if we might save him!"

In the same way, the sinner's degraded condition moves the compassions of his divine Father to their very depths. When the Lord passes by and sees him lying in his blood in the open field (see Ezekiel 16:4–6), He says, "That is my son! He bears the image of his Maker. *'Though I spoke against him, I earnestly remember him still; therefore My heart yearns for him; I will surely have mercy on him'* (Jer. 31:20)." Sinners should remember that the very fact of their being sinners is the thing that moves God's compassion and pity. Do you say, "I do not see how God can make it consistent with His holiness to pardon and love such a sinner as I am"? I can tell you *how*—because He gave His own Son to die in your place!

8. Christ died for us so that He might save us, not *in*, but *from*, our sins. Therefore, must it not grieve Him exceedingly that we continue in sin? What do you think? Suppose you were to see Jesus face-to-face, and He were to show you those wounds in His hands and in His side, and were to say, "I died for you because I saw you lost beyond hope, and because I wanted to save you from your sins. Now, will you repeat those sins again? Can you go on any longer in sin against Me?"

9. You may infer from our subject that Jesus must be willing to save you from the wrath of God, if you truly repent and accept Him as your Savior. How can you doubt it? After He has suffered to the point of death for this purpose, surely the only thing that remains for you to do is to meet the conditions, and you are saved from wrath through Him.

10. You may also infer that God, having not spared His Son, will also with Him freely give you all things (Rom. 8:32). He will give you enough grace to meet all your needs; He will give you the kind care of His providence, the love of His heart, and everything you can need. To continue in sin despite such grace and love is monstrous! It must grieve His heart exceedingly.

A friend of mine who is in charge of one hundred fifty boys in a reform school is accustomed, when they misbehave, to giving them a diet of bread and water for a time. What do you think he does himself in some of these cases? *He puts himself on the same diet of bread and water!* The boys in the school see this, and they learn to love their superintendent and father. Then, when they are tempted to commit a crime, they say to themselves, "If I do wrong, I will have to live on bread and water. But the worst of all is that my father will live on bread and water with me, for my sake. How can I bear that? How can I bear to have my father, who loves me so well, confine himself to bread and water for my sake?"

In the same manner, Jesus put Himself through pain and shame and death so that you might have joy and life—so that you might be forgiven and saved from sinning. Will you go on to sin more? Do you have no heart to appreciate His dying love? Can you possibly go on and sin yet more, when you know of the love shown you on Calvary?

You understand that Christ died to redeem you from sin. Suppose your own eyes were to see Him face-to-face, and He were to tell you all He has done for you. "Sister," He says, "I died to save you from that sin. Will you do it again? Can you go on and sin just the same as if I had never died for you?"

In that reform school of which I spoke, the effects produced on even the worst boys by the love shown them were really striking. The superintendent had long insisted that he did not want locks and bars to confine his boys. The directors had said, "You must lock them in; if you don't, they will run away." On one occasion, the superintendent was to be absent two weeks. A director came to him, urging that he must lock up the boys before he left, for they would certainly run away while he was absent. The superintendent replied, "I think not; I have confidence in those boys." "But," responded the director, "give us some guarantee. Are you willing to pledge the land upon which your house is built, so that if they do run away, the lot goes to the Reform School Fund?" After a little reflection, the superintendent consented, saying, "I will give you my property—and all the property I have in the world—if any of my boys run away while I am gone." Before he set off, he called all the boys together and explained to them his pledge. He asked them to look at his family who depended on him, and then he appealed to their honor and their love for him. "Would you be willing to see me stripped of all my property? I think I can trust you." He left for those two weeks and returned a little unexpectedly and late on one Saturday night. He had scarcely entered the yard when he heard through the sleeping halls, "Our father has come!" And almost in a moment, all the boys were there greeting him and shouting, "We are all here! We are all here!"

Does Christ's love not have as much power as that? The love that the reform school boys have for their official father held them to their place during the long days and nights of his absence; will Christ's love for us not restrain us from sinning? What do you say? Will you say, "If Christ loves me so much, then it is plain He won't send me to hell, and therefore I will go on and sin all I please"? Do you say that? Then there is no hope for you. The Gospel that ought to save you can do nothing for you but sink you deeper in moral and eternal ruin. You are fully determined to pervert it, to your utter damnation! If those reform school boys had said, "Our father loves us so well, he will eat bread and water with us, and therefore we know he will not punish us," would they not certainly bring a curse on themselves? Wouldn't their reformation be utterly hopeless? The same is true of the sinner who can make light of the Savior's dying love. Oh, is it possible that when Jesus has died for you to save your soul from sin and from hell, you can sin again and yet again? Will you live on in sin all the more because He has loved you so much?

Think of this, and make up your mind. Say, "If Christ has died to redeem me from sin, then away with all sinning now and forever. I forsake all my sins from this hour! I can afford to live or to die with my Redeemer—it makes no difference to my eternal state. By God's help, I will have no more to do with sinning forever!"

Chapter 7

On the Atonement

Christ died for our sins according to the Scriptures.
—1 Corinthians 15:3

For He made Him who knew no sin to be sin
for us, that we might become the righteousness
of God in Him.
—2 Corinthians 5:21

But God demonstrates His own love toward us, in that
while we were still sinners, Christ died for us.
—Romans 5:8

The LORD is well pleased for His righteousness' sake;
He will exalt the law and make it honorable.
—Isaiah 42:21

Whom God set forth as a propitiation by His blood,
through faith, to demonstrate His righteousness, because
in His forbearance God had passed over the sins that were
previously committed, to demonstrate at the present time
His righteousness, that He might be just and the justifier
of the one who has faith in Jesus.
—Romans 3:25–26

In this last passage, the apostle Paul stated, with unusual fullness, the theological and philosophical intention of Christ's mission to our world—that is, to set forth before created beings God's righteousness in forgiving sins. It is said here that Christ was *"set forth as a propitiation,"* so that God may be just in forgiving sin. This is based on the assumption that God could not have been just to the universe in forgiving sins unless Christ had been first set forth as a sacrifice.

When we seriously consider the irresistible convictions of our own minds in regard to our relationship to God and His government, we cannot help but see that we are sinners and are lost beyond hope regarding law and justice. The fact that we are grievous sinners against God is an ultimate fact of human consciousness, verified by our irresistible convictions, and as undeniable as the fact that there is such a thing as *wrong*.

Now, because God is holy and good, He must disapprove of wrongdoing, and will punish it. The penalty of His law is pronounced against it. Under this penalty, we stand condemned, and we have no relief except through some adequate atonement—an atonement that is satisfactory to God because it keeps the interests of His kingdom safe. If there were no Bible, we still might know this much with absolute certainty. Even unbelievers are compelled to go this far in their reasoning.

Here we are, then, under absolute and righteous condemnation. Is there any way of escape? If so, it must be revealed to us in the Bible, for it cannot come from any other source. The Bible does claim to reveal a method of escape. This is the great burden of its message.

The Bible opens with a very brief reference to the circumstances under which sin came into the world.

On the Atonement

Without being very detailed as to the *manner* in which sin entered, it is exceptionally full, clear, and definite in showing the fact of sin in the human race. That God regards the human race as being in sin and rebellion is made as plain as language can make it. It is worth noticing that this fact and the connected fact of possible pardon are affirmed on the same authority, and with the same sort of explicitness and clearness. These facts stand or fall together. Evidently, God intended to impress on all minds these two great truths: first, that man is ruined by his own sin; second, that he may be saved through Jesus Christ. To deny the former is to oppose both our own irresistible convictions and God's most explicit revealed testimony. To deny the latter is to shut the door, by our own free will, against all hope of our own salvation.

The philosophical explanations of the Atonement must not be confused with the *fact* of an atonement. Men may be saved by the *fact* if they simply believe it, while they may know nothing about the philosophical explanations. The apostles did not give much explanation, but they asserted the *fact* most earnestly, citing miracles as testimony to prove their authority from God. In this way, they urged men and women to believe the fact and be saved. The fact of the Atonement, then, may be believed unto salvation, and yet the explanation be unknown. This has been the case, no doubt, with thousands of people.

Yet it is very useful to understand the reasons for the Atonement. It often serves to remove skepticism. It is very common for lawyers to reject the fact until they come to see the reasons for the Atonement; once they see this, however, they usually admit the fact. There is a large group of people whose minds also need to see the governmental implications of the Atonement, or they will reject the fact. The reason why the fact is so often doubted is that the explanations given have been unsatisfactory. They have misrepresented God. No wonder men reject them, and along with them, the fact of any atonement at all.

The Perfect Substitute

The purpose of carrying out the penalty of a law is to make a strong impression of the majesty, excellence, and usefulness of that law. The penalty for sin was designed as a testimony to God's regard for the precept of His law, and to His purpose to sustain it. Therefore, an atonement that would answer as a substitute for the infliction of this penalty had to be the sort that would show God's regard for both the precept and penalty of His law. It had to be adapted to enforce obedience. In this respect, its moral power had to be equal to that of the infliction of the penalty on the sinner.

The atonement of Christ is the means used by God's government to sustain His law without carrying out its penalty on the sinner. Of course, it must always be a difficult thing in any government to sustain the authority of law, and the respect due to it, without the execution of penalty. Yet God has accomplished it most perfectly.

Anything that as thoroughly demonstrated the harmfulness and odiousness of sin, God's hatred for it, and His determination to carry out His law in all its demands, could answer as a substitute. The proposed substitute could especially avail if it also made a significant manifestation of God's love to sinners. The Atonement, by the death of Christ, has most emphatically done this.

Let it be distinctly understood that the divine law originated in God's benevolence and has only benevolent intentions. It was revealed solely to promote the greatest possible good, by means of obedience. Such a law can allow for pardon, as long as an expression of penalty can be given that will equally secure obedience—making an equal revelation of the Lawgiver's firmness, integrity, and love. The law being perfect, and being essential to the good of His creatures, God must not set aside its penalty without having some equivalent influence to induce obedience. Consequently, in the Atonement, we find that God has expressed His high regard for His law and for obedience to it.

The Great Representative

In order to make adequate provision for the exercise of mercy to the human race, both the divine and the human had to be united in the person of their Mediator. God and man were both to be represented in the Atonement; the divine Word represented the Godhead, and the man Jesus represented the human race to be redeemed. What the Bible thus asserts is verified in the history of Jesus, for He said and did things that could not have been said and done unless He had been man and also God. On the one hand, He was too weak to carry His cross, through exhaustion of the human body; and on the other, He was mighty to hush the tempest and to raise the dead, through the abundance of divine power. Thus, God and man are both represented in Jesus Christ.

The thing Jesus had to do, then, required that He honor the law and fully obey it; this He did. Standing for the sinner, He had to, in an important sense, bear *"the curse of the law"* (Gal. 3:13). He did not bear the literal penalty, but a vast amount of suffering—an amount that is sufficient, in view of His relationship to God and the universe, to fully demonstrate God's displeasure against sin, and yet His love for both the sinner and all His moral subjects. On the one hand, Jesus represented the human race; on the other, He represented God.

The sacrifice made on Calvary is to be understood as God's offering to public justice, to the general good. God Himself gave up His Son to death, and this Son poured forth His life's blood in expiation for sin, thus throwing open the gates of mercy to a sinning, lost race. This must be regarded as manifesting His love to sinners. This is God's ransom provided for them. Look carefully at the case. The supreme Lawgiver, and indeed the government of the universe, had been ridiculed by rebellion; of course there could be no pardon until this dishonor done to God and His law was thoroughly washed away. This was done by God's free-will offering of His own Son for these great sins.

All of this having been done for you, sinners, what do you think of it? What do you think of the appeal that Paul wrote and God made through him, *"I beseech you therefore, brethren, by the mercies of God, that you present your bodies a living sacrifice, holy, acceptable to God, which is your reasonable service"* (Rom. 12:1)? Think of those mercies. Think of how Christ poured out His life for you. Suppose He were to appear in the midst of you today, holding up His hands dripping with blood, and saying, *"I beseech you...by the mercies of God, that you present your bodies a living sacrifice, holy, acceptable to God."* Would you not feel, by the force of His appeal, that this is a *"reasonable service"*? Wouldn't this love of Christ lead you to fulfill this appeal? What do you think of it? Did He die for all, so that those who live should live not for themselves, but for Him who loved them and gave Himself for them? (See Galatians 2:20.) What do you say?

On the Atonement

The uplifted ax would otherwise have fallen on your neck, but He caught the blow on His own. You could have had no life if He had not died to save it. What will you do? Will you accept this offered mercy or reject it? Will you yield to Him the life that He has spared in such mercy, or will you refuse to yield it?

REMARKS

1. The governmental implications of the Atonement are perfectly apparent. The whole transaction sustains God's law and reveals His love and mercy to sinners. It shows that He is personally ready to forgive, and needs only to have an arrangement made in which His government will not be harmed. What else could so strikingly show His readiness to forgive? He is always ready to pardon, yet He carefully guards against the abuse of it, lest the interests of obedience and happiness be endangered.

2. Why is it so often thought unbelievable that God created such a plan of atonement? Is there anything in it that is unlike God or inconsistent with His revealed character? I doubt whether any moral being can understand this system and still think it incredible. Those who reject it as inconceivable must have failed to understand it.

3. The question might be asked, "Why did Christ die at all, if not for us?" He had never sinned; He did not die on His own account as a sinner; nor did He die as the infants of our sinning race do, with a moral nature that had not yet developed. The only account to be given of His death is that He died not for Himself, but for us.

It might also be asked, "Why did He die in such a way?" He died between two thieves, crushed down beneath a mountainous weight of sorrow. Why was this? Other martyrs have died shouting joyfully; He died in anguish and grief, cast down and agonized as His Father's face was turned away.

All nature seemed to sympathize with His griefs. The sun was clothed in darkness; the earth quaked; the rocks were split apart; all nature was convulsed (Matt. 27:45–54). Even a heathen philosopher exclaimed, "Surely the universe is coming to an end, or the Maker of the universe is dying!" Hear Jesus' piercing cry, *"My God, My God, why have You forsaken Me?"* (v. 46).

Knowing that Christ died as a Savior for sinners, all is plain. He died for the government of God, and He had to suffer these things in order to make a just expression of God's abhorrence of sin. While He stood in the place of guilty sinners, God had to frown on Him and hide His face. This revealed both the spirit of God's government and His own infinite wisdom.

4. Some people have spoken against the Atonement, saying it is likely to encourage sin. But such people neglect the very important distinction between the proper use of a thing and its abuse. No doubt the best things in the universe may be abused, and by abuse they may be perverted to evil—perverted all the more by how much better they are in their legitimate uses.

It would seem that no man can rationally doubt the Atonement's natural goodness. The tendency of manifesting such love, meekness, and self-sacrifice for us is to make the sinner trust and love, and to make him bow before the cross with a broken and contrite heart. But many do abuse it; and the best things, when abused, become the worst. The abuse of the Atonement is the very reason that God sends sinners to hell. He says,

On the Atonement

Anyone who has rejected Moses' law dies without mercy on the testimony of two or three witnesses. Of how much worse punishment, do you suppose, will he be thought worthy who has trampled the Son of God underfoot, counted the blood of the covenant by which he was sanctified a common thing, and insulted the Spirit of grace? (Heb. 10:28–29)

Therefore, if any sinner will abuse atoning blood and trample down the holy law and the very idea of returning to God in penitence and love, God will say of him, *"Of how much worse punishment...will he be thought worthy'* than he who rejected Moses' law and fell beneath its vengeance?"

5. It is a matter of fact that this manifestation of God in Christ does break the hearts of sinners. It has subdued many hearts and will do so to thousands more. If they believe it and hold it as a reality, must it not subdue their hearts to love and grief? Do you not think so? Certainly, if you saw it as it is and felt the force of it in your heart, you would break down this very moment and cry out, "Did Jesus love me so? And will I continue to love sin?" Indeed, your heart would melt as thousands have melted when they have seen the love of Jesus as revealed on the cross.

This is the genuine effect of the sinner's understanding the Gospel and of his giving Jesus Christ credit for His loving-kindness in dying for the lost. Faith thus breaks the stony heart. If this demonstration of God's love in Christ does not break your heart, nothing else will. If this death and love of Christ do not move you to accept Him, nothing else can.

But if you will not set your mind upon it, it will only bring about your ruin. To know this Gospel only enough to reject and disown it can serve no other purpose except to make your guilt greater and your doom more fearful. (See 2 Peter 2:20.)

6. Jesus was made a sin-offering for us. How beautifully this was illustrated by the sin-offerings under the Mosaic system! The animal was brought out to be slain; the blood was carried into the Holy of Holies and sprinkled on the mercy seat. This mercy seat was the sacred cover or lid of the ark that contained the tablets of the Law and other sacred memorials of God's ancient mercies. There they were, those sacred memorials, in that deep recess that no one could enter except the high priest, and he only once a year, on the great Day of Atonement. On this eventful Day, the sacred rites culminated to their highest solemnity. Two goats were brought forward, upon which the High Priest laid his hands and confessed publicly his own sins and the sins of all the people. Then one was driven far away into the wilderness, to signify how God removes our sins as far as the east is from the west (Ps. 103:12). The other goat was slain, and its blood was borne by the high priest into the Most Holy Place, to be sprinkled there upon the mercy seat beneath the golden cherubim. Meanwhile, the vast congregation stood outside, confessing their sins and expecting remission only through the shedding of blood (Heb. 9:22).

When Christ made His ultimate atonement, it was as if the whole world was standing around the base of Calvary, confessing their sins, while Jesus bore His cross to the summit, to hang upon the cross and to bleed and die for the sins of mankind. How fitting that, while Christ is dying, we should be confessing!

Some of you may think it a great thing to go to another country to do missionary work. But Jesus has led the way. He left heaven to do missionary work; He came down to this more-than-heathen world, and no one ever faced such self-denial. Yet He fearlessly met the consequences without the least hesitation. He never shrank from disgrace, from humiliation, or torture. Can you not follow the footsteps of such a leader? Is anything too much for you to suffer, while you follow the lead of such a Captain of your salvation? (See Hebrews 2:10.)

Chapter 8

On Trusting in the Mercy of God

I [will] *trust in the mercy of God forever and ever.*
—Psalm 52:8

In discussing this subject, I will answer the following questions: What is mercy? What is implied in trusting in the mercy of the Lord forever? What are the conditions on which we may safely trust in God's mercy? What mistakes are made on this subject?

What Is Mercy?

Mercy, as an attribute of God, is not to be confused with mere goodness. Goodness naturally and legitimately leads to justice, but mercy is directly opposed to justice. Goodness may demand the exercise of justice—indeed, it often does—but to say that mercy demands the exercise of justice is to misuse the word. Mercy asks that justice be set aside. Thus, mercy and goodness stand in very different relationships to justice and are very different attributes.

Mercy is also a disposition toward pardoning the guilty. Its consists in setting aside the penalty of law when that penalty has been incurred by transgression. As I have said, it is directly opposed to justice. Justice treats every individual according to what he deserves; mercy treats the criminal very differently from how he deserves to be treated. What is deserved is never the rule by which mercy is guided, while it is precisely the rule of justice.

Mercy is exercised only where there is guilt. It always presupposes guilt. The penalty of the law must have been previously incurred, or there can be no purpose for mercy.

Mercy can be exercised no farther than one deserves punishment. It may continue its exercise just as long as punishment is deserved, but no longer. If great punishment is deserved, great mercy can be shown; if endless punishment is due, then there is scope for infinite mercy to be shown, but not otherwise.

What Is Implied in Trusting in the Mercy of God?

A Conviction of Guilt

No one can properly be said to trust in the mercy of God unless he has committed crimes and is conscious of this fact. Justice protects the innocent, and they may safely appeal to it for defense or redress. But for the guilty, nothing remains but to trust in mercy. Trusting in mercy always implies a deep, heartfelt conviction of personal guilt.

No Hope Regarding Justice

Trusting in mercy always implies that we have no hope on the lines of justice. If we had anything to expect from justice, we would not look to mercy. The human heart is too proud to throw itself upon mercy while it presumes itself to have a valid claim to the favors of justice.

Moreover, to appeal to mercy when we might rightfully appeal to justice is never demanded either by God's law or the Gospel, nor can it be in harmony with our relationship to Jehovah's government. In fact, in the nature of the mind, the thing is impossible.

An Understanding of Mercy

Trusting in mercy implies a proper understanding of what mercy is. Many people misunderstand this point because they confuse mercy with grace, which is considered as mere favor to the undeserving. The latter may be shown where there is no mercy, for the term *mercy* is used regarding the pardon of crime. We all know that God shows favor, or grace, in the general sense, to all the wicked on earth. *"He makes His sun rise on the evil and on the good, and sends rain on the just and on the unjust"* (Matt. 5:45). But to trust in this general favor is not the equivalent of trusting in the mercy of God. We never trust in mercy until we really understand what it is—pardon for the crimes of the guilty.

A Belief in God's Mercifulness

Trusting in God's mercy implies a belief that He is merciful. We could not trust Him if we had no such belief. This belief must always lie at the foundation of real trust. Indeed, this belief so naturally leads the soul to reach out to and rest on God—what we call trust—that the New Testament commonly incorporates both meanings (belief and trust) into the word *belief.* Faith, or belief, includes a hearty commitment of the soul to God, and a living trust in Him.

Knowing One's Deserved Punishment

Trusting *"in the mercy of God forever and ever"* implies that one has a conviction of deserving endless punishment. Mercy goes only as far as the punishment that is deserved, and it can go no farther. A prisoner under a three years' sentence to a state prison may ask for mercy in the form of pardon for three years, but he will not ask for a pardon for ten years when he needs it only for three, or ask for a pardon after his three years' term has expired. This principle is perfectly obvious; where punishment is no longer deserved, mercy, and our trust in it, will cease. Yet while one continues to be deserving of punishment, mercy may continue, along with one's trust in it. Therefore, when the psalmist trusted *"in the mercy of God forever,"* he renounced all hope of ever receiving the favor of justice.

An End to Excuses

Trusting in mercy implies a cessation from all excuses and excuse-making. The moment you trust in mercy, you give up all defenses and excuses at once and entirely, for these imply a reliance upon God's justice. An excuse or defense is nothing more than an appeal to justice, a plea designed to justify one's conduct. Trusting in mercy forever implies that one has ceased from all excuses forever.

Thus, a man on trial before a civil court, as long as he pleads justifications and excuses, appeals to justice. But if he goes before the court and pleads guilty, offering no justification or defense whatsoever, he throws himself upon the clemency of the court. This is quite different from self-justification. Sometimes in the courts, the accused party will try both means. He first attempts his own defense; but finding this approach in vain, he shifts his position, confesses his crime, and throws himself upon the mercy of the court.

Now, it is always understood that when a man pleads guilty, he ceases from making excuses, and appeals only to mercy. It is the same in any private matter with one's neighbor. If I justify myself fully, I surely have no confession to make. But if I am conscious of having done him wrong, I freely confess my wrong and appeal to his mercy. Self-justification is directly opposed to confession.

It is also the same in parental discipline. If your child stubbornly justifies himself, he makes no appeal to mercy. But the moment he casts himself upon you with tears and says, "I am all wrong," he ceases to make excuses, and he trusts himself to mercy. And we see that the same principle is true in the government of God. To trust in mercy is to finally give up all reliance on justice. You have no more excuses; you make none.

Conditions of Trusting God's Mercy Forever

Appeasement of Public Justice

The demands of public justice must be satisfied. Public justice looks toward the general good, and if it does not inflict a penalty, it must do what will secure the authority and influence of law in the same way that the infliction of the penalty would do it. It may accept a substitute, as long as the substitute is equally effective in supporting the law and ensuring obedience. God is a great public magistrate, sustaining infinitely responsible relationships to the moral universe. He must be careful what He does.

Perhaps no area of government is more delicate and difficult than the exercise of mercy. It is a critical point. There is eminent danger of making the impression that mercy will trample down law. The very thing that mercy does is to set aside the execution of the *penalty* of law; the danger is that this would seem to set aside the law itself. The great problem is, How can the law retain its full majesty if the execution of its penalty is entirely withdrawn? This is always a difficult and delicate matter.

In human governments, we often see great firmness exercised by the magistrate. During the American Revolution, George Washington was earnestly asked to pardon John André, a British spy. André was an amiable man, and his case aroused a deep sympathy in the American army. Numerous and urgent petitions were made to Washington on his behalf; but no, Washington could not yield. They begged him to see André, hoping that a personal interview might touch his heart; but he refused even to see him. He dared not trust his own feelings. He felt that this was a great crisis, and that a nation's welfare was in peril—hence his stern, unyielding decision. It was not that he lacked compassion of soul; he had a heart to feel. But under the circumstances, he knew too well that no scope must be given to the indulgence of his tender sympathies. He dared not gratify these feelings, lest a nation's ruin should be the result.

Such cases have often occurred in human governments, when every feeling of the soul is on the side of mercy and makes its strong demand for indulgence, but justice forbids.

Often in family government, the parent has an agonizing trial; he would sooner bear the pain himself three times than to inflict it upon his son. But there are more important interests at stake, and the parent must not put those interests in jeopardy by the indulgence of his compassion.

Now, if the exercise of mercy in such cases is difficult, how much more so in the government of God? Hence, the first condition of the exercise of mercy is that something be done to meet the demands of public justice. It is absolutely necessary that law be sustained.

No matter how much God may want to pardon, He is too good to exercise mercy on any conditions that will impair the dignity of His law, give people a license to sin, and open the floodgates of iniquity. Jehovah can never do this. He knows He never ought to.

Regarding this point, it only needs to be said that this difficulty is wholly removed by the atonement of Christ.

Repentance

A second condition is that we repent. Certainly no sinner has the least ground to hope for mercy until he repents. Will God pardon the sinner while he is still in his rebellion? Never. To do so would be most unjust of God—and ruinous to the universe. It would be virtually proclaiming that sin is meaningless—that God is ready to take the most rebellious, unhumbled heart to Himself, no matter how set in wickedness the sinner's heart is. But before God can do this, He must cease to be holy.

Confession of Sins

"Whoever confesses...will have mercy" (Prov. 28:13). Jehovah maintains such a relationship to the moral universe that He cannot forgive without the sinner's confession. He must have the sinner's testimony against himself and in favor of law and obedience.

Suppose a man has been convicted and sentenced to be hung. He petitions the governor for pardon, but he is too proud to confess, at least in public. "May it please Your Honor," he says, "between you and me, I am willing to say that I committed that crime alleged against me, but you must not ask me to make this confession before the world. Will you not have some regard for my feelings and the feelings of my numerous and very respectable friends? Before the world, I will persist in denying the crime. I trust, however, that you will duly consider all the circumstances and grant me a pardon."

The governor would say, "Pardon you? Pardon you, when you are condemning the whole court and jury, accusing them of injustice? Pardon you while you set yourself against the whole administration of justice in the state? Never! You are too proud to take your own place and appear as you are; how can I rely on you to be a good citizen? How can I expect you to be anything better than an arch villain?"

Let it be understood, then, that before we can trust in the mercy of God, we must really repent and make our confession as public as we have made our crime.

Suppose again that a man is convicted and asks for pardon, but will not confess at all. "Oh," he says to the governor, "I have no crimes to confess; I have done nothing particularly wrong. The reason I acted as I did is that I have a desperately wicked heart. I cannot repent and never could. I don't know how it happens that I commit murder so easily. It seems to be second nature to me to kill my neighbor; I can't help it. I am told that you are very good, very merciful; they even say that you are love itself, and I believe it. You surely will grant me a pardon, then, since it will be so easy for you—and it is so horrible for me to be hung. You know I have done only a little wrong, and that little only because I could not help it. You certainly cannot insist upon my making any confession. Can you really have me hung because I don't repent? You certainly are too kind to do any such thing!"

The indignant reply must be, "I don't thank you for your good opinion of me. The law shall take its course; your path is to the gallows!"

Ask the sinner, "Do you repent?" He will mock God by answering, "I don't know about repentance—that is not the question. God is love—God is too good to send men to hell; they slander God who think that He ever sends anybody to hell." Too good! you say; too good! So good that He will forgive whether the sinner repents or not. Too good to hold the reins of His government firmly; too good to secure the best interests of His vast kingdom! Sinner, the God you think of is a being of your own crazy imagination—not the God who built the prison of despair for hardened sinners, not the God who rules the universe by righteous law, and not the God who rules our human race on a gospel system that magnifies that law and makes it honorable.

Restitution

We must really make restitution, as far as it lies in our power to do so. You may see the implications of this in the case of a highway robber. Suppose he has robbed a traveler of $10,000 and is sentenced to prison for life. He petitions for pardon. He is very sorry for his crime and will publicly make any confession that is asked of him. But will he make restitution? No, not he. Perhaps he will give up half of it to the government, so all at once he is vastly patriotic, and liberal besides—ready to make a donation of $5,000 for the public good, ready to consecrate to most benevolent uses a splendid sum of money. But *whose* money is it? Where is his justice to the man he has robbed? What a wretch he is, to consecrate to the public what he has torn from his neighbor and to put it into the treasury of the government! Such a gift would burn right through the treasury! What would you think if the government were to plot such an abominable scheme? You would abhor their detestable corruption.

Consider a man of the world whose whole business career is a course of defrauding. He slyly thrusts his hands into his neighbors' pockets and thus fills up his own. His rule is to sell for more than a thing is worth and to buy for less. He knows how to monopolize and make high prices, and then sell out his accumulated stock. His mind is forever trying to manage and make good bargains. But at last this man must prepare to meet God. So he turns to his money to make it answer all things. He has a large gift for God. Perhaps he will build a church or send a missionary—something sizable to buy a pardon for a life about which his conscience is not very easy. Yes, he has a splendid bribe for God. But will God take it? Never! God burns with indignation at the thought. (See Malachi 3:8.) How shameful to think of stealing from your brother and giving to God! This is not merely robbing Peter to pay Paul, but robbing man to pay God! The pardon of your soul cannot be bought in such a way!

Reformation

Another condition is that we really reform. Suppose there is a villain in your neighborhood who has become the terror of the surrounding region. He has already murdered a score of defenseless women and children. He burns down your houses by night, plunders and robs daily, and every day you hear about another of his crimes. No one feels safe for even a moment. He is purely a villain. At last he is arrested, and you all breathe more easily. Peace is restored. But having received a sentence of death, this miscreant asks for pardon. He shows no repentance whatsoever and does not even make a promise of amending his ways, yet the governor is about to give him a free pardon. If he does it, who will not say, "The governor himself ought to be hung by the neck until he is dead"? But what does the sinner say? He says, "I trust in the great mercy of God. I have nothing to fear."

But does he reform? No. What good can the mercy of God do him if he does not reform?

Justification of the Law

Another condition of trusting in God's mercy is that you must go the whole length in justifying the law and its penalty. Imagine a convicted criminal who doesn't believe that government has any right to take life for any crime. He utterly objects to the justice of such a proceeding, and on this ground insists that he must have a pardon. Will he get it? Will the governor take a position that is flatly opposed to the very law and constitution he has sworn to sustain? Will he crush the law to save one criminal, or even a thousand criminals? Not if he has the spirit of a ruler in his heart. The guilty man, if he desires to have mercy from the executive, must admit the rightness of the law and of the penalty. Otherwise he arrays himself against the law and cannot be trusted in the community.

Now, think of the sinner's case. He has much to say against the ill he deserves and against the justice of eternal punishment. He denounces the laws of God as cruelly and unrighteously severe. Sinner, do you suppose God can forgive you while you pursue such a course? He would as soon repeal His law and vacate His throne. You make it impossible for God to forgive you.

Submission to Government

No sinner can be a proper object of mercy who is not entirely submissive to all the measures of the government that have brought him to conviction.

Suppose a criminal pleads that there has been a conspiracy to waylay and arrest him, that witnesses have been bribed to give false testimony, that the judge has

charged the jury falsely, or that the jury has given an un-
righteous verdict. Could he hope to get a pardon by such
false allegations? Surely not. Such a man cannot be
trusted to sustain law and order in a community under
any government, human or divine.

But the sinner similarly complains and objects.
"Why," he says, "did God allow sin and temptation to
enter this world at all? Why does God let the sinner live
at all, if he will only incur a doom so dreadful? And why
does God block up the sinner's path by His providence,
and cut him down in his sins?" Yet this same sinner talks
about trusting in God's mercy, while all the time he is
accusing God of being an infinite tyrant and of seeking to
crush the helpless, unfortunate sinner! What do these
objections mean? What are they but the uplifted voice of
a guilty rebel accusing his Maker of doing good and
showing mercy to His own rebellious creatures? It needs
only a moment's thought to see that the temptation
complained of is only a good thing placed before a moral
agent in order to melt his heart by love. Yet the sinner
murmurs against this and pours out his complaints
against God.

Be assured that unless you are willing to go the full
length of justifying all that God does, He never can give
you pardon. God has no option to pardon a self-justifying
rebel. The interests of myriads of moral beings forbid His
doing it. When you will fully take the ground of justifying
God and condemning yourself, you will place yourself
where mercy can reach you, and then it surely will—but
not before then.

Unity with the Plan of Salvation

You must wholeheartedly unite with the plan of
salvation. This plan is based on the assumption that we

deserve everlasting death and must be saved, if ever, by sovereign grace and mercy. Nothing can save but mercy—mercy that meets the sinner in the dust, prostrate, without an excuse or a defense, giving to God all the glory and taking to himself all the guilt and shame. There is hope for you, sinner, in embracing this plan with all your heart.

Common Mistakes

Trusting in Justice

Many people really trust in justice and not in mercy. They say, "God is just; He will do me no injustice. I intend to do as well as I can, and then I can safely leave myself in the hands of a just God." True, God will do you no injustice. You never need to fear that. But how terrible if God were to do you strict justice! How fearful if you get no mercy! If God does not show you infinite mercy, you are forever lost, as surely as you are a sinner! This trusting in God's justice is a fatal mistake. The sinner who can do it calmly has never seen God's law and his own heart. The psalmist did not say, "I trust in the justice of God forever and ever."

Individuals who plead for mercy often really rely on justice. The deep conviction of sin does not sink into their souls until they realize what mercy is and feel that they can rely on nothing else.

Not Fulfilling the Conditions

Many people claim to trust in the mercy of God without fulfilling the conditions on which mercy can be shown. They may hold on in such trusting until they die—but no longer.

Sinners do not consider that God cannot excuse them from fulfilling these conditions. He has no right to do so. They spring out of the makeup of His government, from His nature, and must therefore be strictly fulfilled. Sooner than put aside their fulfillment, God would send the whole human race, even the whole universe, to hell. If God were to set aside these conditions and forgive a sinner while he remains unhumbled, impenitent, and unbelieving, He would upset His throne, convulse the moral universe, and kindle another hell in His own self.

Self-justification

Many are defeating their own salvation by self-justification. Pleas that excuse self, and objections that accuse God, stand fully in the way of pardon. Since the world began, it has not been known that a sinner has found mercy in this state.

Thinking We Are Punished Here

Many people pretend to trust in mercy who claim that they are being punished for their sins as they go along. They hope for salvation through mercy, and yet they believe they are being punished for all their sins in this life. Two more absurd and self-contradictory things were never put together. Punished as much as they deserve here, and yet saved through mercy! Why don't they just yell it out that they will be saved after death through justice? Surely if they are punished all they deserve as they go along, justice will ask no more after death.

Covering Up Sins

Some people are covering up their sins, yet dream of going to heaven. Do they think they can hide those sins from the Omniscient Eye? Do they think they can cover their sins and yet prosper, despite God's awe-inspiring Word (Prov. 28:13)?

On Trusting in the Mercy of God

Asking for "Extra" Mercy

We cannot reasonably ask for mercy beyond our acknowledged and felt guilt. Those who suppose that they can do so make a fatal mistake. Without a deep conviction of conscious guilt, we cannot be honest and in earnest in asking for mercy. A man who thinks that sin is something trivial and that its deserved punishment is a small affair may be heard praying, "O Lord, I need a little mercy, only a little. My sins have been few and of little consequence. Grant me, Lord, exemption from the brief and slight punishment that my few errors and defects may have deserved."

You might also hear the Universalist praying, "O Lord, You know that I have been punished for my sins as I have gone along. I have had a fit of sickness and various pains and losses, nearly or quite enough to punish me for all the sins I have committed. Now, therefore, I pray You to give me salvation through Your great mercy." How astonishing that sane men believe such nonsense!

How can a Universalist pray at all? What should he pray for? Not for pardon, for Universalists believe they have a valid claim to exemption from punishment on the lines of justice, as the criminal has who has served out his sentence in the state prison. The only rational prayer that can be made is that God will do them justice and let them off, since they have already been punished enough. But why should they pray for this? God may be trusted to do justice without their praying for it. I don't wonder that Universalists pray very little; what have they to pray for? Their daily bread? Very well. But in their system, they do not need the mercy of God, for they suffer all they deserve. This is a pleasing delusion—it is flattering enough to human pride—but how strange and horribly destructive for rational minds!

Mercy can have no place in any system of Universalism. Every form of this system arrays God in robes of justice—inflexible, fearful justice—yet these men say that they trust in the mercy of God! But what have they done with the Gospel—with all that the Bible says about free pardon to the guilty? They have thrust it out of the Bible. And what have they given us instead? Only justice—punishment enough for sin in this world, or at least in a few years of purgatory. Sin is made to be a trivial thing, government a mere farce, God a liar, and hell imaginary and a fraud! What is all this but the most extreme blasphemy that ever came from hell?

If we ask for only a little mercy, we will get none at all. This may seem strange, but is no less true. If we are to get anything, we must ask for great blessings. Suppose a man deserves to be hung, and yet he asks for only a little favor. Can he be forgiven? No. He must confess his guilt in its full and awful form, and show that he feels it in his very soul. In the same way, sinner, you must come and confess your whole guilt as it is, or you will receive no mercy. Get down low, lower, infinitely low before God, and take mercy there.

Listen to the Universalist. All he can say at first is, "I thank God for a thousand things." But he begins to doubt whether this is quite enough. Perhaps he needs a little more punishment than he has suffered in this life— he sees a little more guilt in himself—so he prays that God will let him off from ten years of deserved punishment in hell. And if he sees a little more guilt, he asks for a reprieve from so much more of his deserved punishment. If truth flashes upon his soul and he sees his own heart and life in the light of Jehovah's law, he gets down lower and lower, as low as he can, and pours out his prayer that God will save him from the eternal hell that he deserves. "Oh," he cries out, "can God forgive so great a sinner?" Yes, and the more you humble yourself, and the more mercy you ask for, the more readily He will forgive you. Take such a position before God so that He can meet you. Recall the Prodigal Son, and his father running, falling on his neck, weeping, welcoming, forgiving! Oh, how that father's heart gushed with tenderness!

It is not the greatness of your sins, but your pride of heart, that forbids your salvation. It is not anything in your past life, but it is your present state of mind, that makes your salvation impossible. Think of this.

You do not need to wait to try to persuade God to save you. He is already trying to persuade you to be saved. You act as if God can hardly be moved by any possible entreaties to exercise mercy. Oh, you do not see how His great heart beats with compassion and presses the streams of mercy forth in all directions, pouring the river of the waters of life at your feet, creating such an appeal to your heart that you have to brace yourself against it, lest you should be persuaded to repent. God would gladly persuade you and break your heart in repentance, so that He may bring you where He can reach you with forgiving mercy—where He can come and bless you without giving up His throne!

To deny that you are deserving of endless punishment is to render your salvation utterly impossible. God never can forgive you on this ground, because you are trying to be saved on the lines of justice. Even if you were to murder every man you meet, you could not make your damnation more certain. You tie up the hands of Mercy and will not let her pluck you from the jaws of death. It is as if your house is on fire and yet you seize your loaded rifle to shoot down every man who comes with his bucket of water to help you. You stand your ground amid the raging element until you sink beneath the flames. Who can help you?

What is that man doing who is trying to make his family believe Universalism? It is as if he would shoot his rifle at the heart of Mercy every time she comes in view. He seems determined to drive off Mercy, and for this purpose uses all the weapons of Universalism and throws himself into the citadel of this *"refuge of lies"* (Isa. 28:17)! Oh, what a work of death this is! Mercy will not reach him or his family; he seems determined, and Mercy cannot come. See how she bends from heaven. Jehovah smiles in love. See how Mercy weeps in pity and holds out the pierced hands of the Crucified One. "But no!" you say. "I don't deserve the punishment; away with the insult of a pardon offered through mere mercy!" What can be more fatal, more damning, more ruinous to the soul?

You see very clearly why not all are saved. It is not because God is not willing to save all, but because they defeat the efforts God makes to save them. They give themselves over to every possible deception; they resist every conviction of guilt, and they repel every call of mercy. What ails those young men and women? What are they doing? Has God come down in His red wrath and vengeance, that they should oppose Him with all their might? Oh, no, He has only come in mercy—this is all—and they are fighting against His mercy, not His vengeance. If this were His awful arm of vengeance, you would bow down or break beneath its blow. But God's mercy comes in its soft whispers (if you would only realize it)—it comes to win your heart.

But you band yourselves together to resist the calls of God's mercy. What are you doing? You invent a thousand excuses; you run together to talk, and talk away all solemn thought; you run to some unbeliever or Universalist to find relief for an uneasy conscience. Ah, sinner, this can do you no good. You flee from God—why? What's the matter? Is God pouring down the floods of His great wrath? No, no; but Mercy has come, and would gladly gather you under her outspread wings where storms of wrath can never come. But no, the sinner pleads against it—runs, fights, rejects the angel of mercy—dashes from his lips the waters of life.

Sinner, this scene will soon come to an end. The time is short. Soon God comes. Are you going to die, my young friend? Are you ready? "Oh, I don't know; I am in great pain. How can I live so? But even more, how can I die? I can't attend to it now—it's too late—too late!" Indeed, young man, you are in weakness now. God's finger has touched you. Oh, if I could only tell you some of the deathbed scenes I have witnessed—if I could make you see them, and hear the deep wailings of unutterable agony as the soul quivered, shuddered, and was swept down swiftly to hell! Those are the very men who ran away from mercy! Mercy could not reach them, but death did. Death seizes its victim. He drags the frightened, shrieking soul to the gateway of hell. That soul falters—groans—what unearthly groans—and he is gone! The sentence of execution has gone out and there is no reprieve. That sinner would not accept mercy when he could have; now he cannot when he wants to. All is over now.

Dying sinner, you may just as well have mercy today as not. All your past sins present no obstacle at all if you will only repent and take the offered pardon. Your God offers you life. *"'For I have no pleasure in the death of one who dies,' says the Lord GOD. 'Therefore turn and live!'"* (Ezek. 18:32). Why will you reject such offered life? If there ever was anything that filled the universe with astonishment, it is the sinner's rejection of mercy. Angels were astonished when they saw the Son of God made flesh, and when they saw Him nailed to a tree. How much more now to see the guilty sinner, doomed to hell, yet spurning offered pardon! What do they see? They see the sinner putting off and still delaying and delaying still, until—what? Until the last curtain falls and the great bell tolls, tolls, tolls the awful knell of the sinner's eternal death!

Where is that sinner? Follow him—down he goes, weeping, wailing, along the sides of the pit. He reaches his own final home; he is in *"his own place"* (Acts 1:25) now and forevermore! Mercy followed him to the last verge of the precipice, and could follow no longer. She has done her part.

What if a spirit from glory should come and speak to you for five minutes? Perhaps it is a relative of yours, perhaps your mother; what would she say? Or a spirit from that world of despair—if such a one could give utterance to the awful realities of that prison house, what would he say? Would he tell you that the preacher has been telling you lies? Would he say, "Don't be frightened by these made-up tales of horror?" Oh, no, but he would tell you that the half has not been told to you and never can be. How that spirit would urge you, if he might, to *"flee from the wrath to come"* (Matt. 3:7)!

Chapter 9

Christ, Our Advocate

❖

If anyone sins, we have an Advocate with the Father,
Jesus Christ the righteous. And He Himself is the
propitiation for our sins, and not for ours only
but also for the whole world.
—1 John 2:1–2

T he Bible abounds with analogies to government. These are designed for our instruction; but if we receive instruction from them, it is because there is a real analogy in many points between the government of God and human governments. Let's examine some of the similarities between the two by answering the following questions: What is an advocate? What are the purposes for which an advocate may be employed? In what sense is Christ the Advocate of sinners? What are the implications of His being their Advocate? What are the essential qualifications of an advocate under such circumstances? What is Christ's plea on behalf of sinners?

What Is an Advocate?

What is the meaning of the term *advocate* when it is used to express a governmental office? An advocate is one who pleads the cause of another, who represents another and acts in his name. An advocate uses his influence on behalf of another at his request.

Why Is an Advocate Needed?

What are some reasons why an advocate may be employed?

1. To secure justice, in case any question involving justice is to be tried.

2. To defend the accused. If one has been accused of committing a crime, an advocate may be employed to conduct his trial on his behalf—to defend him against the charge, and to prevent his conviction if possible.

3. To secure a pardon, when a criminal has been justly condemned and is under sentence. That is, an advocate may be employed either to *secure justice* for his client, or to *obtain mercy* for him, in case he is condemned. The advocate may be employed to prevent his conviction, or when convicted, may be employed in setting aside the execution of the law upon the criminal.

Christ as the Sinner's Advocate

What is the sense in which Christ is the Advocate of sinners? Christ is employed to plead the cause of sinners, but not at the bar of justice. He does not have to defend them against the charge of sin, because the question of their guilt is already settled. The Bible represents them as *"condemned already"* (John 3:18), and every sinner knows this to be true. Every sinner in the world knows that he has sinned, and that consequently he must be condemned by the law of God. This office, then, is exercised not at the bar of justice, but at the throne of grace, at the footstool of sovereign mercy. Christ is employed, not to prevent the *conviction* of the sinner, but to prevent his *execution;* not to prevent his being condemned, but, since he is already condemned, to prevent his being *damned.*

The Implications

What are the implications of Christ being the Advocate of sinners?

1. Christ is employed at the throne of grace and not at the bar of justice. He pleads for sinners, for those who have an established charge against them. This implies that the guilt of the sinner is already ascertained, that the verdict of guilty has been given, that the sentence of the law has been pronounced, and that the sinner awaits his execution.

2. His being appointed by God as the Advocate of sinners implies a merciful disposition in God. If God had not been mercifully disposed toward sinners, no Advocate would have been appointed, and no question of forgiveness would have been raised.

3. It also implies that the exercise of mercy is possible, on certain conditions. Not only is God disposed to be merciful, but it is possible for Him to manifest this disposition in the actual pardon of sin. If this had not been the case, no Advocate would have been appointed.

4. It implies that there is hope, then, for the condemned. Sinners are prisoners; but in this world they are not yet prisoners of despair, but are *"prisoners of hope"* (Zech. 9:12).

5. It implies that there is a governmental necessity for the intervention of an advocate, that the sinner's character is such that he cannot be allowed to plead his

own cause in his own name. He is condemned; he is no longer on trial. In this respect, he is under sentence for a capital crime; consequently, he is an outlaw, and the government cannot recognize him as being capable of performing any legal act. His relationship to the government forbids him to appear before God in his own name, or in his own person. As far as his own personal influence with the government is concerned, he is as a dead man—he is *civilly* dead. Therefore, he must appear by his next friend,* or by his advocate, if he is to be heard at all. He may not appear in his own name and in his own person, but must appear by an advocate who is acceptable to the government.

The Qualifications of the Sinner's Advocate

What are the essential qualifications of an advocate under such circumstances?

1. He must be the uncompromising friend of the government. Observe: Christ appears before the government to pray that mercy will be extended to the guilty party whom He represents. Of course, He must not Himself be the enemy of the government of whom He asks so great a favor, but He should be known to be the devoted friend of the government whose mercy He prays may be extended to the guilty.

2. He must be the uncompromising friend of the law that has been dishonored. The sinner has greatly dishonored, and by his conduct denounced, both the law and the Lawgiver. By his uniform disobedience, the sinner has proclaimed, in the most emphatic manner, that the law is not worthy of obedience and that the Lawgiver is a tyrant. Now, the Advocate must be a friend to this law; He

---

* A *next friend* is one who acts for the benefit of one lacking full legal capacity.

must not sell himself to the dishonor of the law or consent to its dishonor. He must not condemn the law so as to place the Lawgiver in a position in which, if He should set aside the penalty and exercise mercy, He would consent to the dishonor of the law, and by a public act Himself condemn the law. The Advocate seeks to dispense with the execution of the law; but He must not offer, as a reason, that the law is unreasonable and unjust. For in this case, He renders it impossible for the Lawgiver to set aside the execution without consenting to the assertion that the law is not good. In that case, the Lawgiver would condemn Himself instead of the sinner. It is plain, then, that the Advocate must be the uncompromising friend of the law, or He can never secure the exercise of mercy without involving the Lawgiver Himself in the crime of dishonoring the law.

3. Christ as our Advocate must be righteous; that is, He must be clear of any association in the crime of the sinner. He must have no fellowship with the crime; there must be no charge or suspicion of guilt resting upon the Advocate. Unless He Himself is clear of the crime of which the criminal is accused, He is not the proper person to represent him before a throne of mercy.

4. He must be the compassionate friend of the sinner—not of his sins, but of the sinner himself. This distinction is very plain. Everyone knows that a parent can be greatly opposed to the wickedness of his children, while he has great compassion for their persons. He is not a true friend to the sinner who really sympathizes with his sins. Several times I have heard sinners say, as an excuse for not being Christians, that they have many dear friends who are opposed to their becoming Christians and obeying God. Their friends desire them to live on in their sins. They do not want them to change and

become holy, but desire them to remain in their worldly-mindedness and sinfulness. I tell such people that those are their friends in the same sense that the Devil is their friend.

Would they call the Devil their good friend, their kind friend, because he sympathizes with their sins and wishes them not to become Christians? Would you call a man your friend who wished you to commit murder or robbery, to tell a lie, or to commit any crime? Suppose he comes to you and, because you are his friend, desires you to commit some great crime. Would you regard that man as your friend?

No! No man is a true friend of a sinner unless he desires that he abandon his sins. If any person wants you to continue in your sins, he is the adversary of your soul. Instead of being in any proper sense your friend, he is playing the Devil's part to ruin you.

Now, observe that Christ is the compassionate Friend of sinners, a Friend in the best and truest sense. He does not sympathize with your sins, but His heart is set upon saving you from them. As the compassionate Friend of sinners, His compassion must be stronger than death (see Song of Solomon 8:6), or He will never meet the needs of the case.

5. Another qualification must be that He is able sufficiently to honor the law that sinners have dishonored by their transgression. He seeks to avoid the destruction of the dishonored law of God. The law, having been dishonored by sin in the highest degree, must be honored by its being carried out on the criminal; otherwise, the Lawgiver must in some other way bear testimony in favor of the law, before He can justly set aside the execution of its penalty. The law is not to be repealed; the law must not be dishonored. It is the law of

God's nature, the unalterable law of His government, the eternal law of heaven, the law for the government of moral agents in all worlds, in all time, and to all eternity. Sinners have poured contempt upon it by utterly refusing to obey it. Now sin must not be treated lightly—this law must be honored.

God might display the greatness of His glory by carrying out the penalty of law upon all those who have despised it. This would be the solemn testimony of God to sustain its authority and vindicate its claims. If our Advocate appears before God to ask for the remission of sin, so that the penalty of this law may be set aside and not carried out, the questions immediately arise, "But how will the *dishonor* of this law be avoided? What will compensate for the reckless and blasphemous contempt with which this law has been treated? How will sin be forgiven without apparently making light of it?"

Sin has placed the whole question in such a light that God's testimony must in some way be borne against sin, and must sustain the authority of this dishonored law.

It is only fitting that the Advocate of sinners provides Himself with a plea that will meet this difficulty. He must meet this need, if He wishes to secure the setting aside of the penalty. He must be able to provide an adequate substitute for its execution. He must be able to do what will as effectively bear testimony in favor of the law and against sin, as the execution of the law upon the criminal would do. In other words, He must be able to meet the demands of public justice.

6. He must be willing to volunteer His services. From the viewpoint of justice, He cannot be called upon to volunteer a service, or to suffer for the sake of sinners. He may willingly volunteer His services and they

may be accepted; but if He does volunteer His services, He must be able and willing to endure whatever pain or sacrifice is necessary to meet the case.

If the law must be honored by obedience; if *"without shedding of blood there is no remission"* (Heb. 9:22); if an emphatic governmental testimony must be borne against sin, and in honor of the law; if Christ must become the Representative of sinners, offering Himself before the whole universe as a *"propitiation for our sins"* (1 John 2:2), He must be willing to meet the case and make the sacrifice.

7. He must have a good plea. In other words, when He appears before the mercy seat, He must be able to present considerations that will really meet the necessities of the case, and that will make it safe, proper, honorable, and glorious for God to forgive.

Christ's Plea on the Sinner's Behalf

Now, what is the plea of Christ on behalf of sinners?

1. It should be remembered that the appeal is not to justice. Since the fall of man, God has suspended the execution of strict justice upon the human race. To us, as a matter of fact, He has sat upon a throne of mercy. Mercy, and not justice, has been the rule of His administration ever since men were involved in sin.

This is simple fact. Men do sin, and they are not cut off immediately and sent to hell. The execution of justice is suspended, and God is represented as seated upon a throne of grace, or upon a mercy seat. It is here at the mercy seat that Christ carries out the office of Advocate for sinners.

2. Christ's plea for sinners cannot be that they are not guilty. They are guilty and condemned. No question

can be raised regarding their guilt and their deserved punishment; such questions are already settled. It has often appeared strange to me that men overlook the fact that they are *"condemned already"* (John 3:18) and that no question regarding their guilt or their deserved punishment can ever be raised.

3. Christ as our Advocate cannot, and need not, plead a justification. A plea of justification admits the fact charged, but asserts that under the circumstances the accused had a right to do as he did. Christ can never make this plea. This is entirely out of place, the case having been already tried, and the sentence passed.

4. He may not plead anything that will bring condemnation upon the law. He cannot plead that the law was too strict in its precept, or too severe in its penalty; in that case He would not really plead for mercy, but for justice. He would plead in that case that no injustice might be done to the accused. For if He suggests that the law is not just, then the sinner does not deserve the punishment; hence, it would be unjust to punish him, and His plea would amount to the sinner not deserving to be punished. But if this plea should be allowed to prevail, it would be a public acknowledgment on the part of God that His law is unjust. But this may never be.

5. He may not plead anything that will condemn the administration of the Lawgiver. If He were to plead that men had been treated harshly by the Lawgiver—either in their creation, or by His providential arrangements, or by allowing them to be so tempted—or if, in any way, He were to bring forward a plea that condemns the Lawgiver in Creation or in the administration of His government, the Lawgiver could not listen to His plea. He could not forgive the sinner without condemning Himself. In that case, instead of insisting that the sinner should repent,

the Lawgiver would virtually be called upon Himself to repent.

6. He may not plead any excuse whatsoever for the sinner in order to lessen his guilt or the seriousness of his conduct. For if He does, and the Lawgiver should forgive in answer to such a plea, the Lawgiver would confess that He had been wrong and that the sinner did not deserve the sentence that had been pronounced against him.

He must not plead that the sinner does not deserve the damnation of hell, for this plea would virtually accuse the justice of God, and would be equivalent to begging that the sinner might not be sent unjustly to hell. This would not be a proper plea for mercy, but rather an issue with justice. It would be asking that the sinner might not be sent to hell, not because of the mercy of God, but because the justice of God forbids it. This will never be.

7. But Christ may plead His sin-offering as fulfilling a condition upon which we may be forgiven and the law not be compromised. This offering is not to be regarded as the ground upon which justice demands our forgiveness. Our Advocate does not point to this offering as payment, in the sense that justice will now allow Him to *demand* that we be set free. No. As I said before, it is simply the fulfilling of a condition upon which it is safe for the mercy of God to set aside the execution of the law in the case of the penitent sinner.

Some theologians appear to me to have been unable to see this distinction. They insist that the atonement of Christ is the ground of our forgiveness. They seem to assume that He *literally* bore the penalty for us in such a sense that Christ now no longer appeals to *mercy,* but demands *justice* for us. To be consistent, they must maintain that Christ does not plead at a mercy seat for us, but having paid our debt, appears before a throne of justice, and demands our release.

I cannot accept this view. I insist that His offering cannot touch the fact that we intrinsically deserve damnation. His appeal is to the infinite mercy of God, to His loving disposition to pardon; and He points to His atonement, not as demanding our release, but as fulfilling a condition upon which our release is honorable to God. His obedience to the law and the shedding of His blood are seen as a substitute for the execution of the law upon us—in short, Christ may plead the whole of His work as God-man and Mediator. Thus He may give us the full benefit of what He has done—all that He did to sustain the authority of law and to vindicate the character of the Lawgiver—as fulfilling conditions that have made it possible for God to be just and still justify the penitent sinner.

8. But the plea is directed to the merciful disposition of God. He may point to the promise made to Him in Isaiah 52:13–53:2:

Behold, My Servant shall deal prudently; He shall be exalted and extolled and be very high. Just as many were astonished at you, so His visage was marred more than any man, and His form more than the sons of men; so shall He sprinkle many nations. Kings shall shut their mouths at Him; for what had not been told them they shall see, and what they had not heard they shall consider. Who has believed our report? And to whom has the arm of the LORD been revealed? For He shall grow up before Him as a tender plant, and as a root out of dry ground. He has no form or comeliness; and when we see Him, there is no beauty that we should desire Him.

171

9. He may also plead that He becomes our surety, that He undertakes for us, that He is our wisdom, righteousness, sanctification, and redemption. He may point to His infinite fullness, willingness, and ability to restore us to obedience, and to equip us for the service and enjoyments of heaven. It is said that He is made the *"surety of a better covenant"* (Heb. 7:22) than the legal one—a covenant *"established on better promises"* (Heb. 8:6).

10. He may urge as a reason for our pardon the great pleasure it will give God to set aside the execution of the law. *"Mercy triumphs over judgment"* (James 2:13). Judgment is *"his strange [awesome, NKJV] work"* (Isa. 28:21 KJV), but *"He delights in mercy"* (Mic. 7:18).

It is said that *"there is joy in the presence of the angels of God over one sinner who repents"* (Luke 15:10). Do you not think that it gives God the sincerest joy to be able to forgive the wretched sinner and to save him from the doom of hell? He has no pleasure in our death. (See Ezekiel 18:32.)

It grieves Him to be obliged to carry out His law on sinners; and no doubt it gives Him infinitely higher pleasure to forgive us than it does us to be forgiven. He knows full well what are the unutterable horrors of hell and damnation. He knows the sinner cannot bear them. He says, *"'Can your heart endure, or can your hands remain strong, in the days when I shall deal with you?'* (Ezek. 22:14). And what will you do when I punish you?" Our Advocate knows that to punish the sinner is something in which God has no delight—that God will forgive with all His heart.

And do you think such an appeal to the heart of God, to His merciful disposition, will have no avail? It is said of Christ, our Advocate, that *"for the joy that was set before Him* [He] *endured the cross, despising the shame"*

(Heb. 12:2). So great was the love of our Advocate for us that He regarded it a pleasure and a joy so great to save us from hell—a pleasure and joy so great that He counted the shame and agony of the cross as trivial matters. He *despised* them.

This, then, tells us about the heart of our Advocate. Surely He may assume that it will give God the sincerest joy, eternal joy, to be able honorably to grant us a pardon.

11. Christ may point to the glory that will overflow to the Son of God for the part that He has taken in this work.

Will it not be eternally honorable in the Son to have advocated the cause of sinners, to have undertaken at so great expense to Himself a cause so desperate, and to have carried it through at the expense of such agony and blood? Will not all of creation forever wonder and adore as they see this Advocate surrounded with the innumerable throng of souls for whom His advocacy has prevailed?

12. Our Advocate may plead the gratitude of the redeemed, and the profound thanks and praise of all good beings.

Do you not think that the whole family of virtuous beings will forever feel obliged for the intervention of Christ as our Advocate, and for the mercy, patience, and love that has saved all mankind?

REMARKS

1. You see what it is to become a Christian. It is to employ Christ as your Advocate by committing your

cause entirely to Him. You cannot be saved by your works, by your sufferings, by your prayers, or in any way except by the intervention of this Advocate. *"He always lives to make intercession for* [you]" (Heb. 7:25), and He proposes to undertake your cause. To be a Christian is to at once surrender your whole cause, your whole life and being, to Him as your Advocate.

2. He is an Advocate who loses no causes. Every cause committed to Him, and kept in His hands, is infallibly gained. His advocacy is all-prevalent. God has appointed Him as an Advocate; and wherever He appears on behalf of any sinner who has committed his cause to Him, every word of His is sure to prevail.

3. Hence, you see the safety of believers. Christ is always at His post, ever ready to attend to all the concerns of those who have made Him their Advocate. *"He is also able to save to the uttermost those who come to God through Him"* (Heb. 7:25), and you are forever safe if you abide in Him.

4. You see the position of unbelievers. If you are an unbeliever, you have no advocate. God has appointed an Advocate, but you reject Him. You think you can get along without Him. Perhaps some of you think you will be punished for your sins, and you do not ask for forgiveness. Others of you may think you will approach in your own name, and, without any atonement, or without any advocate, you will plead your own cause. But God will not allow it. He has appointed an Advocate to act on your behalf, and unless you approach through Him, God will not hear you.

Outside of Christ, God is to you *"a consuming fire"* (Heb. 12:29). When the Judgment arrives, and you appear in your own name, you will surely appear unsaved and unsanctified. You will not be able to lift up your head, and you will be ashamed to look in the face of the Advocate, who will then sit both as Judge and Advocate.

5. I ask, Have you, by your own consent, made Him your Advocate? It is not enough that God has appointed Him to act in this capacity. He cannot act for you unless you individually commit yourself and your case to His advocacy. This is done, as I have said, by confiding or committing the whole question of your salvation to Him.

6. Do any of you say that you are *unable* to employ Him? Remember, the fee that He requires of you is your heart. You have a heart. It is not money, but your heart, that He seeks. The poor, then, may employ Him as well as the rich; the children, who have not a penny of their own, as well as their rich parents. Everyone may employ Him, for everyone has a heart.

7. He offers His services gratuitously to all, requiring nothing but confidence, gratitude, love, and obedience. These responses the poor and the rich alike must render; these they are both *able* to render.

8. Can any of you do without Him? Have you ever considered how it will be with you? But the question comes now to this: Will you agree to give up your sins and trust your soul to the advocacy of Christ? Will you give Him the fee that He asks—your heart, your confidence, your grateful love, your obedience?

Will He be your Advocate or will He not? Suppose He stood before you now, and in His hands He held the Book of Life and a pen dipped in the light of heaven. Suppose He were to ask, "Who of you will now agree to make Me your Advocate?" Perhaps He asks you, sinner, "Can I be of any service to you? Can I do anything for you, dying sinner? Can I befriend and help you in any way? Can I speak a good word for you? Can I intervene with My blood, My death, My life, My advocacy, to save you from the depths of hell? Will you agree? Shall I take down your name? Shall I write it in the Book of Life? Shall it today be told in heaven that you are saved? And may I report that you have committed your cause to Me, and thus give joy in heaven? Or will you reject Me, stand upon your own defense, and attempt to carry your cause through at the solemn Judgment?"

Sinner, I warn you in the name of Christ not to refuse His advocacy. Agree here and now, and let it be written in heaven.

9. Have any of you made His advocacy sure by committing everything to Him? If you have, He has attended to your cause, because He has secured your pardon; and you have the evidence in your peace of mind. Has He attended to your cause? Do you have the inward sense of reconciliation, the inward witness that you believe that you are forgiven, that you are accepted, that Christ has undertaken for you, that He has already prevailed and secured pardon for you, and that He has given you the peace of God that passes understanding (Phil. 4:7)? It is a striking fact in Christian experience that, whenever we really commit our cause to Jesus, He without delay secures our pardon and gives us the assurance of our acceptance. In the inward peace that follows, we know that He has intervened by His blood, that His blood is accepted for us, that His advocacy has prevailed, and that we are saved.

Do not stop short of this. If your peace is truly made with God—if you are in fact forgiven—then the sting of remorse is gone; there is no longer any strife or any irritation between your spirit and the Spirit of God. The sense of condemnation and remorse has given place to the spirit of gospel liberty, peace, and love.

The stony heart is gone; the heart of flesh has taken its place (see Ezekiel 36:26), and peace flows like a river.

Do you have this? If so, then leave your cause, by a continual committal of it, to the advocacy of Christ. If you abide in Him, and let Him abide in you, you will be as safe as the surroundings of almighty arms can make you.

Chapter 10

The Gathering of the Great Harvest

*But when He saw the multitudes, He was moved
with compassion for them, because they were weary
and scattered, like sheep having no shepherd. Then
He said to His disciples, "The harvest truly is plentiful,
but the laborers are few. Therefore pray the Lord of
the harvest to send out laborers into His harvest."*
—Matthew 9:36–38

In discussing this subject, we will consider the following questions: To whom is this precept addressed? What does it mean? What is implied in the prayer required? I will also show that an indispensable condition of salvation is a state of mind that is obedient to this precept.

To Whom Is This Precept Addressed?

Beyond question, the precept of the above Scripture is addressed to all who are under obligation to be benevolent—all beings upon whom the law of love is imposed. Consequently, it is addressed to all human beings, for all who are human bear moral responsibility—they ought to care for the souls of their fellowmen, and of course they fall under this requirement.

Note the occasion of Christ's remarks. He was travelling among the cities and villages of His country, *"teaching in their synagogues, preaching the gospel of the kingdom, and healing all kinds of sickness and all kinds of disease among the people"* (Matt. 4:23). He saw multitudes before Him—mostly in great ignorance of God and salvation—and His deeply compassionate heart was moved, *"because they were weary and scattered, like sheep having no shepherd."* Alas! They were perishing for lack of the Bread of Heaven, and who should go and break it to their needy souls?

His feelings were all the more affected because He saw that they felt hungry. They not only were starving for the Bread of Life, but they seemed to have some consciousness of the fact. They were just then in the condition of a harvest field, the white grain of which is ready for the sickle and awaits the coming of the reapers. The multitudes were ready to be gathered into the granary of the great Lord of the Harvest. No wonder this sight touched the deepest compassions of His benevolent heart.

The Meaning of This Precept

What is really intended by the precept, *"Pray the Lord of the harvest to send out laborers into His harvest"*? Every precept relating to external conduct has its spirit and also its letter. The letter refers to the *external,* but the spirit to the *internal.* Yet both are involved in real obedience. In the present case, the letter of the precept requires prayer. But this does not mean that merely using the words of prayer is real obedience. Besides the words, there must be a praying state of mind. The precept does not require us to lie and play the hypocrite before God. No one can for a moment suppose this to be the case. Therefore, it must be admitted that the precept requires the spirit of prayer as well as the letter. It requires, first, a praying state of mind, and then also its due expression in the forms of prayer.

What, then, is the true spirit of this precept? I answer, love for souls. Certainly it does not require us to pray for men without any heart in our prayer, but rather to pray with a sincere heart, full of real love for human welfare—a love for immortal souls and a deep concern for their salvation. It undoubtedly requires the same compassion that Jesus Himself had for souls. His heart was gushing with real compassion for dying souls, and He was conscious that His own state of mind was right. Therefore, He could do no less than require the same state of mind of all His people. Hence, He requires that we should have real and deep compassion for souls, compassion that really moves the heart, for this is obviously what His compassion was.

This involves a full commitment of the soul to this purpose. Christ had committed His soul to the great work of saving men; for this He labored and toiled; for this His heart agonized; for this His life was ready to be offered. Therefore, He could do no less than require the same of His people.

Again, an honest offering of this prayer implies a willingness to let God use us in His harvest field in any capacity He pleases. When the farmer gathers his harvest, many things are to be done, and often he needs many hands to do them. Some he sends in to cut the grain, others to bind it; some gather into the barn, and others glean the field, so that nothing will be lost. In the same way, Christ has a variety of jobs for His servants in the great harvest field, and no one can be of real use to Him unless he is willing to work in any department of the Master's service, thankful for the privilege of doing the humblest service for such a Master and in such a cause.

Hence, when we engage in honest prayer for this purpose, it implies that we are really committed to the work, and that we have given ourselves up most sincerely and entirely to do all we can for Christ and His cause on earth. We are always on hand, ready for any labor or any suffering. For if we do not have this mind, we need not think that our prayers will do any good. It would be a sorry and insulting prayer to say, "Lord, send somebody else to do all the hard work, and let me do little or nothing." Everybody knows that such a prayer would only insult God.

Hence, sincere prayer for Christ's cause implies that you are willing to do anything you can do to promote its interests, devoting all your powers and resources for this purpose. You may not withhold even your own children. Nothing will be too dear for you to offer on God's altar.

Suppose a man were to give nothing—to withhold all his means and suppress all efforts, except that he says he will pray. Indeed, he claims that he prays. But do you suppose that his prayer has any heart in it? Does he mean what he says? Does he love the cause of Christ more than all other things? Truly, he does not. You never could say that a young man does all he can for Christ's harvest if he refuses to go into the field to work. Nor could you say that an aged, but wealthy, man is doing all he can if he refuses to give anything to help support the laborers in the field.

The Gathering of the Great Harvest

The Implications of Obedience

What, then, is implied in really obeying this precept?

1. The first implication is a sense of personal responsibility regarding the salvation of the world. No man ever begins to obey this command who does not feel a personal responsibility to take this as his own work. He must really feel, "This is my work for life. For this I am to live and spend my strength." It does not matter whether you are young enough to go abroad into the foreign field, or whether you are qualified for the gospel ministry; you must feel such a sense of responsibility that you will cheerfully and most heartily do all you can. You can chop wood or draw water, even if you cannot take on more responsible tasks. An honest and consecrated heart is willing to do any sort of work, to bear any sort of burden. Unless you are willing to do anything you can wisely and successfully do, you will not comply with the conditions of a prayerful state of mind.

2. Another implication of obeying this command is a sense of the value of souls. You must see that souls are precious—that their guilt is fearful while they remain in unpardoned sin, and that their danger is most appalling. Without such a sense of the value of the interests at stake, you will not pray with fervent, strong desire; and without a proper understanding of their guilt, danger, and remedy, you will not pray in faith for God's intervening grace. Indeed, you must have so much of the love of God—a love like God's love for sinners—in your soul that you are ready for any sacrifice or any labor. You need to feel as God feels. He *"so loved the world that He gave His only begotten Son, that whoever believes in Him should not perish but have everlasting life"* (John 3:16). You need to love the world in such a way that your love

will lead you to make similar sacrifices and put forth similar labors.

Each servant of God must have love for souls—the kind of love that God had in giving up His Son to die, and that Christ had in coming down cheerfully to make Himself the offering—or his prayers for this purpose will have little heart and no power with God. This love for souls is always implied in acceptable prayer—prayer that God would send forth laborers into His harvest. I have often thought that the reason why so many pray only in form and not in heart for the salvation of souls is that they lack this love—this love of God—for the souls of the perishing.

3. Acceptable prayer for this purpose implies confidence in the ability, wisdom, and willingness of God to push this work forward. No man can pray for what he supposes may be opposed to God's will, or beyond His ability, or too complicated for His wisdom. If you ask God to send forth laborers, the prayer assumes that you trust in His ability to do the work well, and in His willingness to press it forward in answer to prayer.

4. The very idea of prayer implies that you understand this to be a part of the divine plan—that Christians should pray for God's intervening power and wisdom to carry forward this great work. You do not pray until you see that God gives you the privilege, commands the duty, and encourages it by assuring you that it is an essential condition of His using His power to give success. It is said in the Scriptures, *"I will also let the house of Israel inquire of Me to do this for them"* (Ezek. 36:37).

5. Again, no one complies with the spirit of this condition who does not pray with all his might—fervently and with great perseverance and urgency—for the blessing. He must feel the pressure of a great cause;

moreover, he must feel that it cannot prosper without God's intervening power. Pressed by these considerations, he will pour out his soul with intensely fervent supplications.

6. Unless the church is filled with the spirit of prayer, God will not send forth the laborers into His harvest. Plainly, the command to pray for such laborers implies that God expects prayer and will wait until it is made. The prayer comes into His plan as one of the appointed means, and cannot be set aside. Undoubtedly, it was in answer to prayer that God sent out such a multitude of strong men after the Ascension. It is obvious that prayer and the special hand of God brought in a Saul of Tarsus and sent him forth to call in whole tribes and nations of the Gentile world. And many others were called along with him. *"The Lord gave the word; great was the company of those who proclaimed it"* (Ps. 68:11).

7. That this prayer should be made in faith, resting in assurance on God's everlasting promise, is too obvious to need proof or illustration.

8. Honest, sincere prayer implies that we lay ourselves and all we have upon His altar. We must feel that this is our business and that our strength and resources are to be used to carry out this work. Therefore, only when we are given up to the work can we honestly ask God to raise up laborers and press the work forward. When a man's lips say, "Lord, send forth laborers," but his life proclaims, "I don't care whether a man goes or not; I'll not help the work to go forward," you know that he is only playing the hypocrite before God.

By this I do not imply that every honest servant of Christ must feel that he is called to the ministry and must enter it—by no means. God does not call every pious man into this field; He has many other fields and labors that are essential parts of the great whole. The thing I have to say is that we must be ready for any part that God's providence assigns us.

When we can go and are in a situation to obtain the necessary education, then the true spirit of the prayer in our text implies that we pray that God would send *us*. If we are in a condition to go, then this prayer plainly implies that we have the heart to beg the privilege for ourselves, that God would put us into His missionary work. Then we will say with the ancient prophet, *"Here am I! Send me"* (Isa. 6:8).

Do you not suppose that Christ expected His disciples to go, and to *desire* to go? Did He not assume that they would pray for the privilege of being put into this precious trust? How can we be in real sympathy with Christ unless we love the work of laboring in this Gospel harvest, and long to be commissioned to go forth and put in our sickle with our own hand? Most certainly, if we were in Christ's spirit we would say, *"I have a baptism to be baptized with, and how distressed I am till it is accomplished!"* (Luke 12:50). We would cry out, "Lord, let me go! Let me go, for dying millions are just now perishing in their sins." How can I ask God to send out others if I am unwilling to go myself? I have heard many say, "Oh, if only I were young! How I would rejoice to go myself!" This seems like a state of mind that can honestly pray for God to send forth laborers.

9. The spirit of this prayer implies that we are willing to make any personal sacrifices in order to go. Aren't men always willing to make personal sacrifices in order to gain the great object of their heart's desire? Was there never a merchant, seeking pearls, who found one of great value and was quite willing to go and sell all that he had and buy it? (See Matthew 13:45–46.)

10. Moreover, an honest heart before God in this prayer implies that you are willing to do all you can to prepare yourselves to accomplish this work. Each young man or young woman should say, "God requires something of me in this work." It may be that God wants you as a servant in some missionary family. If so, you are ready to go. No matter what the work may be, no labor done for God or for man is degrading. In the spirit of this prayer, you will say, "If I may only wash the feet of my Lord's servants, I will thoroughly enjoy it." All young people especially, feeling that life is before them, should say, "I must devote myself, in the most effective way possible, to the promotion of my Savior's cause." Suppose a man bows his soul in earnest prayer before God, saying, "O Lord, send out hosts of men into this harvest field." Does this not imply that he prepares himself for this work with his might? Does it not imply that he is ready to do the utmost he can in any way whatsoever?

11. Again, this prayer, when made honestly, implies that we do all we can to prepare others to go out. Our prayer will be, "Lord, give us hearts to prepare others and to get as many ready as possible and as well prepared as possible for the gathering in of this great harvest."

12. Of course, it is also implied that we abstain from whatever would hinder us, and that we make no arrangements that would tie our hands. Many young Christians do this, sometimes heedlessly, often in a way that shows that they are by no means fully set to do God's work before all other work.

When we honestly pray to God to send out laborers, and our own circumstances allow us to go, we are to expect that He will send us. What? Does God need laborers of every description, and will He not send *us*? Count on it; He will send out the man who prays in a right way and whose heart is deeply and fully with God. And we do not need to suspect that God will lack the wisdom to manage His matters well. He will put all His men where they should be, into the fields they are best qualified to fill. The good reaper will be put into his post, sickle in hand; and if there are feeble ones who can only glean, He will put them there.

When young people have health and the means for obtaining an education, they must assume that God calls them to this work. They should assume that God expects them to enter the field. They must focus upon this work as their own. Thinking of the masses of God's true children who are lifting up this prayer, "Lord, send forth laborers to gather in the nations to Your Son," they will surely infer that the Lord will answer these prayers and send out all His true, equipped, and faithful men into this field. Most assuredly, if God has given you the mind, the training, the tact, the heart, and the opportunity to get all the necessary preparation, you may know that He will send you forth. You say, "Is it possible that I am prepared, ready, and waiting, and that the church is praying that God would send laborers forth, and yet He will not send me?" Impossible!

One indispensable part of this preparation is a *heart* for it. God does not want workers in His harvest field whose hearts are not there. You would not want workmen in your field who have no heart for their work. Neither does God. But He expects us to have this preparation. And He will not accept the excuse from any man that he has no heart to engage in this service. The lack of a heart for this work is not your misfortune, but your fault, your great and damning sin.

This brings me to my next general proposition, that this state of mind is an indispensable condition of salvation.

The Gathering of the Great Harvest

A Necessary Condition of Salvation

Many people in the church are dreadfully in the dark about the conditions of salvation. I was once preaching on this subject, urging that holiness is one condition of salvation *"without which no one will see the Lord"* (Heb. 12:14), when I was confronted and vehemently opposed by a doctor of divinity. He said, "The Bible makes faith the sole and only condition of salvation. Paul preached that faith is *the* condition, and plainly meant to exclude every other condition." But I answered, "Why did Paul press so earnestly and hold up so prominently the doctrine of salvation by faith? Because he had to oppose the great Jewish error of salvation by works. Such preaching was greatly needed *then,* and Paul met the emergency. But when Antinomianism* developed, James was called out to equally uphold the doctrine that faith without works is dead—that good works are the legitimate fruit of living faith and are essential evidence of its life and genuineness. This at once raised a new question about the nature of gospel faith. James taught that all true gospel faith must work by love. It must be an affectionate, childlike confidence that draws the soul into sympathy with Christ and leads it forward powerfully to *do* all His will."

Many professing Christians believe that nothing is necessary but simply faith and repentance, and that faith may exist without real benevolence, and consequently without good works. No mistake can be greater than this. The grand requirement that God sets upon man is that he become truly benevolent. This is the essence of all

---

* Antinomians believe a heretical doctrine that, by grace, Christians are set free from the obligation to obey the moral law, especially the Ten Commandments. To Antinomians, faith alone is necessary for salvation.

true religion: a state of mind that has compassion like God's compassion for human souls, that cries out in earnest prayer for their salvation, and that does all it can to accomplish this purpose. Therefore, if true religion is a condition of salvation, then the state of mind set forth in our text is also a condition.

REMARKS

1. This compassionate state of mind is required of sinners as well as saints. All men ought to feel this compassion for others' souls. Why should they not? Can any reason be named why a sinner should not feel as much compassion for souls as a Christian, or why he should not love God and man as ardently?

2. Those who claim to be believers but who do not obey the true spirit of these precepts are hypocrites, without one exception. They claim to be truly religious, but are they? Certainly not, unless they are on the altar, devoted to God's work, and sincerely sympathizing with it in their hearts. Without this, every one of them is a hypocrite. You claim to have the spirit of Christ, but when you see the multitudes as He saw them, perishing for lack of gospel light, do you cry out in mighty prayer with compassion for their souls? If you do not have this spirit, consider yourself a hypocrite.

3. Many do not pray that God will send forth laborers because they are afraid He will send *them*. When religion was repulsive to me, I feared that if I were converted, God would send me to preach the Gospel. But I thought further about this subject. I said, "God has a right to use me as He pleases, and I have no right

to resist. If I do resist, He will put me in hell. If God wants me to be a minister of His Gospel and I resist and rebel, He surely ought to put me in hell, and undoubtedly He will."

But there are many young men and women who never give themselves to prayer for the conversion of the world, lest God should send them into this work. Perhaps you would be embarrassed to pray, "Lord, send forth laborers, but don't send me." If the reason you don't want to go is that you have no heart for it, you may consider yourself a hypocrite. There is no mistake about this.

If you say, "I have a heart for the work, but I am not qualified to go," then you may know that God will not call you unless you are or can be qualified. He does not want incompetent men in the service of His kingdom.

4. With sorrow I am compelled to say that many people don't care whether the work is done or not. It is obvious that they do not sympathize with Jesus Christ in this cause.

Beloved, do you sympathize with your great Leader? I can never read our text verses without being affected by the manifestation they make of Christ's tenderness and love. There were the thronging multitudes before Him. To the merely external eye, all might have seemed pleasant; but to One who thought of their spiritual state, there was enough to move the deep fountains of compassion. Christ saw them scattered abroad as sheep who have no shepherd. They had no teachers or guides in whom they could place their confidence. They were in darkness and moral death. Christ wept over them. He called on His disciples to sympathize with their case and to unite with Him in mighty prayer that the Lord of the Harvest would send forth laborers. Such was His spirit. And now, dear reader, do you care whether or not this work is done?

5. Many seem determined to shirk this labor and leave it all for others to do. Indeed, they will hardly entertain the question of what part God wants them to take and perform. Now let me ask you, Will these individuals be welcomed and applauded in the end with the words, *"Well done, good and faithful servant....Enter into the joy of your* [L]*ord"* (Matt. 25:21)? Never!

6. Many say, "I am not called," but really they are not devoted to this work at all, so they do not care whether they are called or not. They do not *want* to be called—not they!

It is painful to see that many are committing themselves in some way against the work. They are putting themselves in a position that forbids their engaging in it. But let me ask you, dear reader, can you expect ever to be saved if, when you have the power and the means to engage in this work, you have no heart for it? No, indeed! You knock in vain at the gate of the blessed! You may go there and knock, but what will be the answer? "Are you my faithful servants? Were you among the few—faithful among the faithless—quick and ready at your Master's call? Oh, no, you were determined to shun the labor and to shirk the self-denial! I do not know you! Your portion lies outside the city walls!"

Let no one offer the excuse that he has not been called, for God calls *everyone* to some sort of labor in the great harvest field. You never need to excuse yourself as one not called to some service for your Lord and Master. And let no one excuse himself from the ministry unless he himself is praying and longing to go, yet God, through His providence, is calling him to some other part of the great labor.

Many will be sent to hell for treating this subject as they have, with so much selfishness of heart. I know the feelings of a young man who for a long time struggled between a strong conviction that God has called him to the ministry and a great resistance to engaging in this work. I know what these feelings are, for I felt them a long time myself. For a long time, I had a secret conviction that I should be a minister, though my heart resisted it. In fact, my conversion centered very much upon my giving up this fight with God, and subduing this resistance against God's call.

7. You can see what it is to be a Christian, and what God demands of men at conversion. The turning point is this: Will you really and honestly serve God? Consider the case of students in college. With students the question is likely to be, Will you abandon all your ambitious schemes and devote yourself to the humble, unambitious toil of preaching Christ's Gospel to the poor? Most students are ambitious and aspiring; they have plans to elevate themselves in this world, and it is difficult for them to renounce these plans. Hence, their being saved will depend much, perhaps entirely, on their giving themselves up to this work in the true gospel spirit of self-denial.

8. Many have been called to this work who afterwards backslide and abandon it. They begin well but backslide; they fall into a state of great perplexity about their duty. Perhaps they are so unwilling to see their duty and so eager to evade it that God will not struggle with them any longer, but gives them up to their covetousness and their ambition.

Are you earnestly crying out, *"Lord, what do You want me to do?"* (Acts 9:6)? Be assured, God wants you in His field somewhere; He wants you in it, but He wants you first to repent and prepare your heart for the gospel ministry. You need not enter it until you have done this.

Many are waiting for a miraculous call. This is a great mistake. God does not call men in any miraculous way. The finger of His providence points out the path, and He prepares you for the work you are to do. You do not need to fear that God will call you wrong. He will point out the work He wants *you* to do. Therefore, ask Him to guide you to the right spot in the great field. He will surely do it.

Dear reader, do you say, "O my God, I am on hand, ready for any part of the work You have for me to do"? What do you say? Are you prepared to take this ground? Are you ready to consecrate your all to the work of your Lord? Do you say, "Yes, God will have all my powers, entirely and forever"? *"I beseech you therefore, brethren, by the mercies of God, that you present your bodies a living sacrifice, holy, acceptable to God, which is your reasonable service"* (Rom. 12:1). The altar of God is before you. A whole sacrifice is the thing required. Are you ready to forsake all your selfish schemes? You who have talents that are suited for the ministry, will you devote them with all your soul to this work? Will you *"deal kindly and truly with my master"* (Gen. 24:49)? Do you love His cause, and consider it your highest glory to be a laborer together with God in gathering the nations of lost men into the fold of your Redeemer?

Chapter 11

The Christian Duty of
Converting Sinners

*Brethren, if anyone among you wanders from the truth,
and someone turns him back, let him know that he who
turns a sinner from the error of his way will save a soul
from death and cover a multitude of sins.*
—*James 5:19–20*

This passage of Scripture brings before us a subject
of present duty and of great practical importance.
So that we may clearly understand it, let us examine some questions concerning its meaning.

What Is a Sinner?

A Moral Agent

A sinner is, essentially, a moral agent. He must be at least this much, whatever else he may or may not be. He must have free will, in the sense of being able to originate his own activities. He must be the responsible author of his own acts, in such a sense that he is not compelled irresistibly to act one way or another, except according to his own free choice.

He must also have intellect, so that he can understand his moral responsibilities. Any creature that lacks this element of character is not a moral agent and cannot be a sinner.

He must also be able to be moved to action—so that he can be influenced toward voluntary activity. He also must have a capacity to take hold of the motives for right or wrong action.

These are the essential elements of the mind necessary to constitute a moral agent. Yet these are not all the characteristics that develop in a sinner.

A Selfish Being

The sinner is a selfish moral agent devoted to his own interests, making himself his own supreme end of action. His own interests, not the interests of others, are his chief concern. Thus, every sinner is a moral agent, acting under this law of selfishness, having free will and all the powers of a moral agent, but making self the great end of all his action.

One Who Errs

We have here the true idea of sin. Sin, in an important sense, is error. A sinner is one who errs. Our text says, *"He who turns a sinner from the error of his way."* Sin is not merely a mistake, for mistakes are made through ignorance or inability. Nor is sin a mere defect of one's physical makeup, attributable to its Author. It is an *"error of his way."* It is missing the mark in his voluntary course of conduct. It is a voluntary divergence from the line of duty. It is not an innocent mistake, but a reckless yielding to impulse. It involves a wrong purpose—a bad intention—a being influenced by appetite or passion, in opposition to reason and conscience. It is an attempt to

196

secure some present gratification at the expense of resisting convictions of duty. This is most emphatically *missing the mark*.

What Is Conversion?

What is it to "[turn] *a sinner from the error of his way*"? This error lies in his having a wrong purpose of life—his own present worldly interests. Hence, to convert him from the error of his ways is to turn him from this course to a benevolent consecration of himself to God and to human well-being. This is precisely what is meant by conversion. It is changing the great moral end of action. It puts benevolence in the place of selfishness.

How Does One Convert a Sinner?

Our text verse reads, *"If anyone among you wanders from the truth, and someone turns him back"*—implying that one may convert a sinner. But how can this be done?

I answer, the change must be a voluntary one. It is not a change in the essence of the soul or in the essence of the body—not any change in the created physical makeup. Rather, it is a change that the mind itself, acting under various influences, makes regarding its own voluntary end of action. It is an intelligent change—the mind, acting intelligently and freely, changes its moral course, and does it for perceived reasons.

The Bible ascribes conversion to various agencies:

1. God is spoken of as converting sinners, and Christians pray to God to do so.

2. Christians are spoken of as converting sinners. We see this in our text verse.

3. The truth is also said to convert sinners.

Let it be considered that no man can convert another without the cooperation and consent of that other. His conversion consists in his yielding up his will and changing his voluntary course. He can never do this against his own free will. He may be persuaded and induced to change his voluntary course, but to be persuaded is simply to be led to change one's chosen course and choose another.

Even God cannot convert a sinner without his own consent, for the simple reason that this would be a contradiction. Being converted implies that one gives his own consent; otherwise, it is no conversion at all. Therefore, God converts men only as He persuades them to turn from the error of their selfish ways to the rightness of benevolent ways.

In addition, man can convert a sinner only in the sense of presenting the reasons that bring about the voluntary change and thus persuade him to repent. If he can do this, then he converts a sinner from the error of his ways. But the Bible informs us that man alone never does or can convert a sinner.

It is true, however, that when man acts humbly, depending on God, God works with him and by him. Men are *"labourers together with God"* (1 Cor. 3:9 KJV). They present reasons, and God urges those reasons on the mind. When the minister preaches, or when you converse with sinners, man presents truth, and God causes the mind to see it with great clarity and to feel its personal application with great power. Man persuades and God persuades; man speaks to his ear, and God speaks to his heart. Man presents truth through the medium of his senses to reach his free mind; God presses it upon his mind in order to secure his voluntary yielding to its claims.

The Christian Duty of Converting Sinners

The Bible speaks of sinners as being persuaded: *"You almost persuade me to become a Christian"* (Acts 26:28). In this, the language of the Bible is entirely natural, just as if you were to say you had turned a man from his original purpose, or that your arguments had turned him, or that his own convictions of truth had turned him. So the language of the Bible on this subject is without artificiality, speaking in perfect harmony with the laws of the mind.

What Kind of Death?

What kind of death is meant by the text verse when it reads, *"will save a soul from death"*? Observe that it is a soul, not a body, that is to be saved from death; consequently, we may dismiss all thoughts of the death of the body in this context. However truly converted a man is, his body must nevertheless die.

The passage speaks of the death of the soul. The death of the soul sometimes means *spiritual death,* a state in which the mind is not influenced by truth as it should be. The man is under the dominion of sin and rejects the influence of truth.

Or the death of the soul may be *eternal death*—the utter loss of the soul, and its final ruin. Of course, the sinner is spiritually dead, and if this condition were to continue through eternity, this would become eternal death. Yet the Bible represents the sinner dying unpardoned as *"go*[ing] *away into everlasting punishment"* (Matt. 25:46) and as being *"punished with everlasting destruction from the presence of the Lord and from the glory of His power"* (2 Thess. 1:9). To be always a sinner is awful enough—it is a death of fearful horror—but how terribly worse this is when you imagine it as heightened by everlasting punishment, far away *"from the presence of the Lord and from the glory of His power"*!

Why Is This Important?

Our text verse says, *"He who turns a sinner from the error of his way will save a soul from death."* Consequently, he saves him from all the misery he otherwise would have endured. So much misery is saved—so much that this amount is greater in the case of each sinner saved than all that has been experienced in our entire world up to this hour. This may startle you at first and may seem unbelievable. Yet you have only to consider the matter attentively, and you will see it must be true. That which has no end—which swells utterly beyond all our capacities for computation—must surpass any finite amount, however great.

Yet the amount of actual misery experienced in this world has been very great. As you go about the great cities in any country, you cannot fail to see it. Suppose you could look over an entire continent at once, just to take in all its miseries in one glance. Suppose you could see all forms of human woe and could measure their magnitude—all the woes of slavery, oppression, intemperance, war, lust, disease, heartache. Suppose you could stand above some battlefield and hear all its groans and curses in one ascending volume, and gauge the magnitude of its unutterable woes. Suppose you could hear the echo of its agonies as they roll up to the heavens. You would then say, "There is indeed an ocean of agony here; yet all this is only a drop in the bucket compared with the vast amount, defying all calculation, that each lost sinner must endure, and from which each converted sinner is saved."

The Christian Duty of Converting Sinners

If you were to see a train rushing over a dozen men at once, grinding their flesh and bones, you could not bear the sight. Perhaps you would even faint. But oh, if you could see all the agonies of the earth accumulated, and could hear the awful groans ascending in one deafening roar that would shake the very earth, how your nerves would quiver! Yet all this would be merely nothing compared with the eternal sufferings of one lost soul! And this would be true each moment of this lost soul's existence, no matter how little his comparative suffering.

Furthermore, the amount of suffering thus saved is greater not only than all that ever has been, but also than all that ever will be endured in this world. And this is true, even though the number of inhabitants may be increased a millionfold, and their miseries heightened in proportion. No matter how small the degree of suffering that the sinner would endure, all the earth's miseries cannot begin to approximate the agonies of his lost spirit.

We may also extend our comparison and take in all that has been endured in the universe thus far—all the agonies of earth and all the agonies of hell combined, up to this hour. Yet even this conglomerate is utterly too scanty to approach the amount of suffering saved when one sinner is converted. No—the amount thus saved is greater than the created universe ever can endure in any finite duration. It is even greater, thousands and thousands of times greater, than all finite minds can ever imagine. You may embrace the entire imagination of all finite minds, of every man and every angel, of all minds but that of God, and still the man who saves one soul from death saves, in that single act, more misery from being endured than all this immeasurable amount. He saves more misery, by thousands of times, than the entire universe of created minds can imagine.

I am afraid many of you have never taken the time to think of this subject. You are not to escape from this fearful conclusion by saying that suffering is only a natural consequence of sin, and that there is no governmental infliction of pain. It does not matter at all whether the suffering is governmental or natural. The amount is all I speak of now. If a man continues in his sins, he will be miserable forever by natural law; therefore, the man who converts a sinner from his sins saves all this immeasurable amount of suffering.

Suppose a bird is to remove the whole earth by taking away a single grain of sand once every thousand years. What an eternity, almost, it would take! And yet this would not measure eternity. Now suppose, sinner, that it is you yourself who is suffering during all this period, and that you are destined to suffer until this bird has removed the last grain of sand. Suppose you are to suffer no more intense suffering than you have sometimes felt; yet suppose that the bird must remove, in this slow process, not only this world, but also the whole material universe. Only a single grain at a time!

Or suppose the universe were a million times more extensive than it is, and that you must suffer while the bird removes a single grain from this vast universe once every thousand years. Would it not appear to you like an eternity? Therefore, if you knew that you must be deprived of all happiness for all time, would not the knowledge sink into your soul with a crushing force?

But, after all, this is only an illustration for our understanding. Let the time thus measured roll on, until all is removed that God ever created or ever can create; even so, it scarcely affords a comparison, for eternity has *no end*. You cannot even estimate its end. After the lapse of the longest period you can imagine, you have approached no nearer than you were when you first began. O sinner, *"can your heart endure, or can your hands remain strong, in the days when* [God] *shall deal with you?"* (Ezek. 22:14).

But let us look at still another view of the case. He who converts a sinner not only saves more misery but also provides more happiness than all the world has yet enjoyed, or even all the created universe. Have you converted a sinner? Then think what has been gained! The time will come when he will say, "In my experience of God and divine things, I have enjoyed more than the combined happiness of all creatures during the whole duration of our world; and yet my happiness has only just begun! Onward, still onward—onward forever rolls the deep tide of my blessedness, and evermore increasing!"

Look also at the work in which this converted man is engaged. Just look at it. In some sunny hour when you have caught glimpses of God and of His love, you have said, "If only this might last forever! If only this stormy world were not around me! Oh, if only my soul had *'wings like a dove! I would fly away and be at rest'* (Ps. 55:6)." These were only aspirations for the rest that heaven provides, whereas what the converted man enjoys above *is* heaven. You must add to this the rich and glorious idea of perpetual increase; the converted man's blessedness not only endures forever, but also increases forever. And this is the bliss of every converted sinner.

If these things are true, then the following points are also true.

1. Converting sinners is the work of the Christian life. It is the great work to which we, as Christians, are especially appointed. Who can doubt this?

2. It is the great work of life because its importance demands that it should be. It is so much beyond any

other work in importance that it cannot be rationally regarded as anything less than the great work of life.

3. It can be made the great work of life because Jesus Christ has made provision for it. His atonement covers the human race and lays the foundation so broad that whosoever desires may come. (See Revelation 22:17.) The promise of His Spirit to aid each Christian in this work is equally broad, and was designed to open the way for each one to become a laborer together with God in this work of saving souls.

4. Benevolence can never stop short of it. Where so much good can be done and so much misery can be prevented, how is it possible that benevolence can fail to do its utmost to convert sinners?

5. Living to save others is a condition of saving ourselves. No man is truly converted who does not live to save others. Every truly converted man turns from selfishness to benevolence, and benevolence surely leads him to do all he can to save the souls of his fellowmen. This is the changeless law of benevolent action.

6. Those who are self-deceived live only to save themselves. This is the chief end of all their religion. All their religious efforts and activities tend toward this sole objective. If they are pretty sure of their own conversion, they are satisfied. Sometimes they will sympathize with sinners who are especially near to them, but their selfishness commonly takes them no further in benevolence, unless their concern for their good name and reputation prompts them.

7. Some people put forth no effort to convert sinners, but act as if this were a matter of no consequence whatsoever. They do not work to persuade men to be reconciled to God.

Some seem to be waiting for divine intervention. They make no effort to lead their children or friends to salvation. As if they felt no interest in the great issue, they wait and wait for God or miracle to move. How horrible that they do nothing in this great work of human life!

Many so-called believers have no faith in God's blessing, and so they have no expectation of success. Consequently, they make no effort in faith. Their own experience cannot help them, because never having had faith, they have never had success. Many ministers preach but do no good. Having failed so long, they have lost all faith. They have not done their work expecting success; hence, they have not had success.

Besides ministers, many professing believers seem to have lost all confidence. Ask them if they are doing anything toward the work of converting sinners. They will answer honestly, "Nothing." But if their hearts were full of love for souls or of the love of Christ, they would certainly make efforts. They would at least try to convert sinners from the error of their ways. They would live religion—would hold up its light as a natural, spontaneous thing.

Everyone, male or female, of every age and in any position in life whatsoever, should make it his or her business to save souls. There are, indeed, many other things to be done; everything has its place. But don't neglect the greatest duty of all.

Many professing Christians seem never to convert sinners. Some of you might say, "Under God, I have been the means of saving some souls." But some of you cannot even say this. You know you have never labored honestly and with all your heart for this purpose. And you do not know that you have ever been the means of converting one sinner.

What will I say of you young converts? Have you given yourselves up to this work? Are you laboring for

God? Have you gone to your impenitent friends, even to their rooms, and by personal, affectionate entreaty implored them to be reconciled to God?

In whatever way you are able, have you sought to save souls and do what you can in this work? Have you succeeded?

Suppose all the professing Christians in your church were to do this, each in his or her sphere and each doing all he or she could do. How many would be left unconverted? Imagine if each one were to say, "I lay myself on the altar of my God for this work; I confess all my past delinquencies; from now on, God helping me, this will be the labor of my life." If each one of you were to begin by removing all your old offenses and occasions of stumbling, and were to publicly confess your remissness and every other form of public offense, confessing how little you have done for souls, crying out, "Oh, how wickedly I have lived in this matter! I must reform, must confess, repent, and change the course of my life altogether"—if you were all to do this and then set yourselves in your place, to pluck your neighbor out of the fire, how glorious would be the result!

But to neglect the souls of others and think you will still be saved yourself is one of guilt's worst blunders! For unless you live to save others, how can you hope to be saved yourself? *"Now if anyone does not have the Spirit of Christ, he is not His"* (Rom. 8:9).

Chapter 12

Essential Elements of the Christian Experience

Blessed are those who hunger and thirst for righteousness, for they shall be filled.
—*Matthew 5:6*

There are a great many things in the experience of Christians that, when traced out in their natural history, are exceedingly interesting. I have been surprised at how very common it is to forget about what is characteristic of the Christian experience, while what is merely incidental to Christianity remains and makes up some people's entire idea of what religion is. The way some people talk about their experience leaves you quite in the dark as to its genuineness, even when they propose to give you the reasons of their hope.

The Life of God in the Soul

In this chapter, my first intention is to state some of the facts that belong to the life of God in the soul.

Hunger and Thirst

The *"hunger and thirst"* mentioned in our text verse are states of the mind, not of the body. We all know about the natural, bodily hunger and thirst. Because of our physical makeup, food and drink are necessary to our well-being in the present world. These appetites are normal, and they focus on their appropriate objects.

But the spiritual hunger and spiritual thirst are as truly normal as the natural. It is no more a figure of speech to use the terms *hunger* and *thirst* in this case than in the other. Everyone knows what it is to hunger and thirst for food and drink. This is a matter of fact and experience. Likewise, the spiritual appetites are things of fact and experience, and they are similarly related to the objects that are adapted to their demand.

But let me present the true idea of hungering and thirsting after righteousness. This state of mind is not merely conviction; it is not remorse, or sorrow, or a struggle to obtain a hope or to get out of danger. All these feelings may have preceded, but the hungering after righteousness is none of these. It is a desire to realize the idea of spiritual and moral purity. One has in some measure appreciated the purity of heaven and the necessity of being as pure as the holy ones there, in order to enjoy their bliss and breathe freely in their atmosphere.

When the mind gets a right view of the atmosphere of heaven, it sees plainly that it cannot breathe there, but will be suffocated, unless its own spirit has begun to realize the purity of that world. I remember the case of a man who, after living a Christian life for a season, relapsed into sin. At length, God reclaimed His wandering child. When I next saw him and heard him speak of his state of relapse, he turned suddenly away and burst into tears, saying, "I have been living in sin, almost choked to death in its atmosphere; it seemed as if I could not breathe in it. It almost choked the breath of spiritual life from my system."

Haven't some of you known what this means? You could not bear the infernal atmosphere of sin! After you get out of it, you say, "Let me never be there again!" Your soul agonizes and struggles to find some refuge against this awful relapsing into sin. You long for a pure atmosphere and a pure heart that will never hold fellowship with darkness or its works again. (See Ephesians 5:11.)

The young convert might not at first distinctly understand his own condition and needs. Yet his soul longs for righteousness with irrepressible longings. The now-enlightened convert says, "I *must* be drawn into living union with God as revealed in Jesus Christ. I cannot rest until I find God and have Him revealed to me as my everlasting *'refuge and strength'* (Ps. 46:1)."

Several years ago, I preached a sermon for the purpose of developing the idea of the spiritual life. The minister for whom I preached said to me, "I want to show you a letter written many years ago by a lady now in advanced age, detailing her remarkable experience on this subject." After her conversion, this woman had apparently found herself exceedingly weak spiritually, and often wondered if this was all the stability and strength she could hope for from Christ in His Gospel. She said, "Is this all that God can do for me?" For a long time and with much prayer, she examined her Bible. At last she found that, underlying everything she had ever read and examined before, there lay many passages that revealed the real Gospel—salvation from sinning. She saw the provisions of the Gospel clearly.

This woman then shut herself up in her room, determined to seek this blessing until she found it. Her soul went forth to God, seeking communion with Him and seeking the great blessing that she so deeply felt she needed. She had found the promises in God's Word, and now she held on to them as if she could not let them go until they had all been fulfilled in her own joyful experience. She cried mightily to God, saying, "If You do not give me this blessing, I can never believe You again." In the end, the Lord showed her that the provisions had already been made and were just as full and as glorious as they needed to be or could be. He showed her that she could receive them by faith if she so desired. In fact, it was plain that the Spirit of the Lord was pressing acceptance upon her, so that she had only to believe—to open her mouth wide so that it might be filled (Ps. 81:10). She saw and obeyed; then she became firm and strong. Christ had made her free. She was no longer in bondage; her Lord had absolutely enlarged her soul in faith and love, and she could triumphantly exclaim, "Glory be to God! Christ has made me free."

The state of mind expressed by hungering and thirsting is a real hunger and thirst, and its focus is on the Bread and Water of Life. (See, for example, John 6:35; Revelation 21:6.) These images (if indeed they are to be regarded as images at all) are kept up fully throughout the Bible, and all true Christians can testify to the appropriateness of the language used to express these ideas.

Although the awakened sinner may have agonies and convictions, he has no clear ideas of what union with Christ in conversion is, nor does he clearly comprehend the need for a perfectly cleansed heart. He needs some experience of what holiness is, and often he also seems to need to have tasted some of the bitterness of sin, before he will fully understand this great spiritual need to be made a partaker of Christ's perfect righteousness. This righteousness is not suggested, but something real. It is imparted, not merely suggested. Christ draws the souls of His people into such union with Himself that they become *"partakers of the divine nature"* (2 Pet. 1:4), or as elsewhere expressed, *"partakers of His holiness"* (Heb. 12:10). The tried Christian longs for this. Having had a little taste of it, and then having tasted the bitterness of a relapse into sin, his soul is roused to struggle to realize this blessed union with Christ.

Being Filled with Righteousness

A few words should now be said on what is implied in being filled with this righteousness.

Worldly men incessantly hunger and thirst for worldly things. But attainment never outstrips desire. Hence, they are never filled. There is always a conscious desire that can never be satisfied by any acquisition of worldly good. It is highly remarkable that worldly men can never be filled by the things they seek. The Scripture says that a worldly man's desire enlarges itself as hell, and is never satisfied. (See Habakkuk 2:5.) The more he obtains, the more he really hungers and thirsts.

Let it be especially noted that this being filled with righteousness is not *perfection* in the highest sense of the term. People often use the term *perfection* to describe what is absolutely complete—a state that precludes improvement and beyond which there can be no progress. There can be no such perfection among Christians in any world—earth or heaven. The term can pertain to no being besides God. He, and He alone, is perfect beyond possibility of progress. All other beings are making progress—the wicked from bad to worse, the righteous from good to better. Some people suppose that believers will make no more progress in heaven. But I propose that they will progress geometrically; in other words, the more they have, the farther they will advance.

I have often wondered whether the law of "impulsive progression," which seems to prevail here, will operate in heaven. Let me explain what I mean by impulsive progression. From time to time the mind puts forth great efforts to make attainments in holiness. The attainment having been made, the mind rests for a season, as if it had eaten its meal and awaited the natural return of appetite before eating again. Is it not possible that the same law of progress exists even in heaven?

We see the operation of this law in the usual course of the Christian life. Intense longing and desire bring forth great struggling and earnest prayer; eventually, the special blessing sought is found, and for a time the soul seems to be filled to overflowing. It seems to be fully satisfied and to have received all it supposed possible and perhaps even more than was ever asked or thought. The soul cries out before the Lord, "I did not know there was such fullness in store for Your people. How wonderful that God has granted it to someone like myself!" The soul finds itself swallowed up and lost in the great depths and riches of such a blessing. But soon this individual grows hungry again, and he readies himself for a new struggle.

This is what is sometimes expressed as a baptism, an anointing, a sealing by the Spirit, an earnest of the Spirit. (See, for example, Mark 1:8; 1 John 2:27; 2 Corinthians 1:22 KJV.) All these terms are pertinent and beautiful to denote this special work of the Divine Spirit in the heart.

Those who experience it know that it is aptly described as eating the flesh and drinking the blood of the Lord Jesus (see John 6:48–58), because the soul so truly seems to live on Christ. It is also the Bread and the Water of Life, which are promised freely to him who is hungry and thirsty. (See Revelation 21:6.) These terms may seem very mysterious and meaningless to those who have had no experience, but they are all plain to him who has known in his own soul what they mean. If you ask why figures of speech are used at all to denote spiritual things, you will see that it is the best way for the human mind to understand spiritual things. Christ's language must have seemed very mysterious to His hearers, yet it was the best He could use for His purpose. If any man wants to do God's will, he will understand His doctrine (see John 7:17); but how can a selfish, debased, and disobedient mind expect to enter into the spiritual meaning of this language?

How strange Christ's words must have sounded to the ears of Jewish priests: *"The Spirit...dwells with you and will be in you"* (John 14:17); *"Abide in Me"* (John 15:4)! How could they understand these things? *"I am the bread which came down from heaven"* (John 6:41)—what could this mean to them? They thought they understood about the manna from heaven, and they idolized Moses; but how were they to understand what this Nazarene said about giving them the *"true bread from heaven"* (v. 32)? No wonder they were confused, having only legal ideas of religion, and having not even the remotest approximation of the idea of a living union with the Messiah for the purposes of spiritual life.

Conditions of Receiving This Fullness

Hungering and Thirsting

What are the conditions of receiving this fullness? *"Blessed are those who hunger and thirst for righteousness, for they shall be filled."* The only condition specified in this passage is that the soul must hunger and thirst for it. But we know it is very common for promises to be made in the Bible, and yet for all the conditions of a promise not to be stated in the same context. If we find them elsewhere, we are to regard them as fixed conditions, and they are to be understood as implied where they are not expressed.

Faith

Elsewhere we are told that faith is a fundamental condition of being filled with righteousness. Men must believe for righteousness and receive it by faith (Rom. 3:21–22). This is as necessary as eating bread for the sustenance of the body. Ordinary food must be taken into the system by our own voluntary act. We take and eat; then the system digests the food. In the same way, faith receives and digests the Bread of Life.

In general, before Christians will sufficiently understand the relationship between their needs and the means of supplying them, this hunger and thirst become very intense, so as to overpower and cast into insignificance all their other appetites and desires. Just as one ruling passion throws all minor ones into the shadows, and may sometimes suspend them for a season entirely, so we find that a soul intensely hungering and thirsting after righteousness almost forgets to hunger and thirst even after common food and drink. Place a book before him, and he cannot bring his mind to enjoy it now. Invite him to a concert, and he has no taste for it at present. He longs to find God, and can spare little interest in any other friend at this time. Offer him worldly society, and you will find he takes the least possible interest in it. He knows such companions will not understand what his soul so intensely craves, and of course it would be in vain to look for sympathy in that area.

Essential Elements of the Christian Experience

Understanding What Is Needed

In being filled with righteousness, it is an important condition that the mind should have a somewhat clear understanding of the thing needed and of the means of obtaining it. Effort cannot be well directed unless the subject is in some good measure understood. What is the sealing of the Spirit? What is this baptism? One must see what this is before he can intelligently seek it and hope to gain it. While it is true that no one can know before experience as he can and will know afterwards, he can learn something before and often much more after the light of experience shines upon his soul. There is no more mystery here than there is in hungering for a good dinner, and being refreshed by it after you have eaten it.

Believing the Promises

Again, if we wish to have this fullness of righteousness, we must be sure to believe the promise of it and all the promises like it. We must regard them as truly promises of God—all yes and amen in Christ Jesus (2 Cor. 1:20)—and as reliable as the promise of pardon to those who are penitent and believing.

We must also insist upon the fulfillment of these promises to our souls. We are authorized to expect this in answer to our faith. When we are sure that we ask in sincerity, we should expect the blessing just as we always expect God to be faithful to His Word. Will He not do as He has said? Has He promised but will not perform? (See Romans 4:21.)

We must believe that the promise implies a full supply. Our faith must not limit the power or the grace of Christ. The Christian is not restricted in God. Therefore, let him take care that he does not restrict himself by his narrow ideas of what God can do and loves to do for His hungering and thirsting children.

Often there is need of great perseverance in the search for this blessing. Because of the darkness of the mind and the smallness of its faith, the way may not for a long time be prepared for the full bestowal of this great blessing.

REMARKS

1. The Antinomian Perfectionists misinterpreted the meaning of this and of similar passages. They supposed that whoever believes gets so filled that he or she never thirsts anymore. But the fact is, the mind may rise higher and higher, making still richer attainments in holiness at each level of progress. The mind may indeed find many resting places, just as the pilgrim in Bunyan's *The Pilgrim's Progress* found many resting places: at the top of the hill Difficulty, on the Delectable Mountains, and wherever he passed through scenes of great triumph, great faith, and great joy in God. After these times, there will come other periods of intense desire for new baptisms of the Spirit and for a new ascent upon the heights of the divine life.

This is to be the course of things as long as we remain in the flesh, and perhaps forever. Perhaps the blessed spirits in heaven will always experience new developments of God being made to the mind, and by this means new stages of progress and growth in holiness. When we stand with those heavenly spirits, we will look back over the past and say, "Oh, this everlasting progress—this is indeed the blessedness of heaven!" This will transcend the highest thoughts we had when we looked forward to heaven from the dim distance of our earthly pilgrimage! In heaven there is no end to the disclosures to be made, or to the truths to be learned. For if there were no more food for our souls, how could there be any more spiritual thirst and spiritual hunger? How, indeed, could there be more spiritual joy? Suppose that somewhere in the lapse of heaven's eternal ages, we were to reach a point where nothing more remained to be learned—not another thing to be inquired about, not another fact to be investigated or truth to be known. What a blow this would be to the bliss of heaven!

We are told that the angels desire to look into the things of salvation (1 Pet. 1:12). When they saw our Messiah born, they were allowed to come so near us with their joyous outbursts of praise that even mortals could hear. Do you not suppose those angels, too, are growing in grace and advancing in knowledge? No doubt they are, most wonderfully, and have been ever since they came into being.

How much more they must know of God now than they did before our world was created! And how much more they have yet to learn from God's government over the human race! Do you think they have no more desires for the knowledge of God? And have they no more desire to rise to yet higher conformity of heart and character to the great Model of Heaven?

If this is true with angels, surely it is no less true with their younger brothers—the holy who are *redeemed from among men*" (Rev. 14:4).

You might suppose that, by studying a subject for some time, you would learn all of it. This would be a great mistake. You might master many subjects and still have other heights to ascend—other vast fields of knowledge to explore. You might have the best of human teachers and the best possible opportunities for learning, yet still it would take you many lives to master all there is in even human science. The mind is not made to be so filled that it craves no more or can receive no more. Like the trees planted on the rivers of the waters of life that bring forth twelve kinds of fruits and have roots that go deep and drink largely of those blessed waters, so is the mind that God has endowed with the functions of immortal progress. (See Revelation 22:2.)

What Christian does not find, as he reads the Bible, new and deeper levels of meaning never seen before— new truths revealed and new beauties displayed? An old friend of mine used to say, "I am reading the Word of God. It is deep and rich, like the great heart of its Author. I have read for two hours now and have not gotten past two verses. It will take me for all eternity to read it through." And so it was for him. He really found more in the Bible than other men did. He went deeper, and the deeper he went, the richer he found its precious ores.

The psalmist said, *"Open my eyes, that I may see wondrous things from Your law"* (Ps. 119:18). Have you not been so ravished with love for the blessed Book that you have wanted to clasp it to your chest and become purified with its Spirit? As you have gone down into its depths and found new beauties and new areas of truth to explore in each successive level of its thoughts, have you not been filled with intense desire to live long enough and have time and strength enough to see, to learn, and to enjoy it all? As you ascend the side of a lofty mountain, at each stage you see the landscape spreading out in grander beauty and broader range. Likewise, as you really study the great and rich things of God's spiritual kingdom, there is no limit to the knowledge of God, for the fields only become broader and more enchanting as you ascend. Do you not think that he who eats and drinks and fills his soul with divine righteousness must be truly blessed?

2. I have a strong conviction that some of you, my readers, need a new development of the spiritual life. You need to go deeper into the knowledge of God as revealed in the soul; you need to hunger and thirst more intensely, so that you might be filled as you have not often been. Even though you may have tasted the graciousness of the Lord, you need to eat and drink primarily at His table. It will not do you any good to live on those old dinners, long past and long since digested. You need a fresh meal. It is time for you to say, "I must know more about this being filled with righteousness. My soul longs for this heavenly food. I must come again into this banqueting house, to be feasted again with His love."

3. Once the soul has been filled, it cannot be satisfied to enjoy its rich spiritual provisions alone. If one is well fed himself, he will want to see others fed and blessed also. The Spirit of Christ in his heart is a spirit of love, and this can never rest unless it sees others reaching the same enjoyment that is so delightful to itself.

4. Real Christians should be, and generally will be, growing better and holier as they come closer to heaven. On the other hand, there is a great and fearful contrast between an elderly growing Christian and an elderly sinner growing in depravity and guilt! The one is ripening for heaven, the other for hell. The one goes on praising and loving, laboring and suffering for God and for his generation according to the will of God. The other goes on in his downward course, scolding and cursing as he goes, abhorred by men and disowned by his Maker. You have seen the awful contrast. It might be hard to believe that two men so unlike were both raised in the same

town, taught at the same school, instructed in the same church, and presented with the same Gospel; for one is saved and the other damned.

5. Is it not time that each one of you who has any spiritual life should stand out before the world and *"put on your beautiful garments"* (Isa. 52:1)? Let all the world see that the Gospel contains a power and a glory that human philosophy has never even approached. Show that the Gospel gives birth to purity and peace. Show that it enlarges the heart and opens the hand for the good of all humankind. Show that it conquers selfishness and transforms the soul from hate to love.

Sinners, you who have a great deal of earthly hunger and thirst, let your ears be opened to hear the glad tidings of real salvation. You whose hearts have never known solid peace; you who are forever desiring yet never satisfied (see Habakkuk 2:5); you who cry in your inmost souls for fame, honor, and wealth—here is something far better than all that you seek. Here are durable riches and righteousness. Here are the first installments of pleasures that flow forever at God's right hand. Here is heaven offered and urged upon you for your consideration and your choice. If you will choose life before death, you will make the wisest decision for your eternal well-being.